Sinner Takes All

Sinner Takes All

A Memoir of Love & Porn

TERA PATRICK

with Carrie Borzillo

GOTHAM
BOOKS

GOTHAM BOOKS
Published by Penguin Group (USA) Inc.
375 Hudson Street, New York, New York 10014, U.S.A.
Penguin Group (Canada), 90 Eglinton Avenue East, Suite 700, Toronto, Ontario M4P 2Y3,
Canada (a division of Pearson Penguin Canada Inc.); Penguin Books Ltd, 80 Strand, London
WC2R 0RL, England; Penguin Ireland, 25 St Stephen's Green, Dublin 2, Ireland (a division of
Penguin Books Ltd); Penguin Group (Australia), 250 Camberwell Road, Camberwell, Victoria
3124, Australia (a division of Pearson Australia Group Pty Ltd); Penguin Books India Pvt Ltd,
11 Community Centre, Panchsheel Park, New Delhi—110 017, India; Penguin Group (NZ),
67 Apollo Drive, Rosedale, North Shore 0632, New Zealand (a division of Pearson
New Zealand Ltd); Penguin Books (South Africa) (Pty) Ltd, 24 Sturdee Avenue,
Rosebank, Johannesburg 2196, South Africa

Penguin Books Ltd, Registered Offices: 80 Strand, London WC2R 0RL, England

Published by Gotham Books, a member of Penguin Group (USA) Inc.

First printing, January 2010

1   3   5   7   9   10   8   6   4   2

Photo credits appear on page 287.

LIBRARY OF CONGRESS CATALOGING-IN-PUBLICATION DATA
Patric, Tera, 1976–
Sinner takes all: a memoir of love and porn / Tera Patrick ; with Carrie Borzillo.
p.   cm.
ISBN 978-1-592-40522-0
1.   Patrick, Tera, 1976–2.   Motion picture actors and actresses—United States—Biography.
I.   Borzillo, Carrie. II.   Title.
PN2287.P27A3 2010
791.4302'8092—dc22
[B]   2009040837

Printed in the United States of America

Set in Arrus BT•Designed by Sabrina Bowers

While the author has made every effort to provide accurate telephone numbers and Internet
addresses at the time of publication, neither the publisher nor the author assumes any
responsibility for errors, or for changes that occur after publication. Further, the publisher does
not have any control over and does not assume any responsibility for author or third-party Web
sites or their content.

Penguin is committed to publishing works of quality and integrity.
In that spirit, we are proud to offer this book to our readers;
however, the story, the experiences, and the words
are the author's alone.

I DEDICATE THIS BOOK TO MY SISTER, DEBRA, WHO'S ALWAYS BEEN
MY ROCK, AND MY MOTHER. PREEYA, WHO CAME BACK INTO MY
LIFE OVER THE COURSE OF WRITING THIS BOOK.

Contents

CONTENTS

Foreword

BY MARGARET CHO

I think that porn stars and stand-up comedians have a lot in common. We're both looking for a physical reaction from our audience—bodies flooding with endorphins and people feeling good in the dark. And laughter, like orgasms, can be faked, but it's always better if it isn't. Laughter can feel like short, abbreviated climaxes—orgasms in miniature—and porn, like a good laugh, can make you wet your pants. At least, that is the hope.

Tera Patrick and I have even more in common than the porn/comedy thing. We are both women who decided to go forward and forge our own path, leaving behind a culture that urged women to be silent and subservient. Tera's story and mine are different in the details, but I love hearing about her journey because essentially we both came from the same place—invisibility.

I remember when I was six years old and I came to the bitter understanding that I was not white. Even though I was too young to have seen *The Brady Bunch* in its heyday, I never missed the reruns that played on a seemingly continuous loop on TV after school. I was obsessed with Cindy Brady's blond hair, which glistened like gold ropes on either side of her head. I begged my mother to braid my hair in the same style, but no matter what she did, it never looked the same. I asked my mother why my straight black hair didn't look like spun gold on the shoulders of an angel. She said simply, "Because you don't have blond hair. Because we are not white." This realization was shattering. To know that I didn't look like the people on TV made me think that I would never be on TV. Never seeing anyone like myself out there made me feel like I didn't exist.

In this book you'll learn that when Tera was a little Asian girl, she looked up to a blond goddess of her own: Marilyn Monroe. But what Tera realized even then was that it wasn't Marilyn's blond hair that mattered. It was her power, and the fact that the whole world couldn't stop looking.

When I got older and started doing stand-up comedy, comics and other people in the business warned me about being too sexual: "Don't be sexy. Be cute." I never understood that. People always thought I was sexy, and I talked a lot about sex onstage, so why was it wrong to have people want to have sex with me? I am glad for it every time it happens. I came to understand that people viewed women's sexuality, especially an empowered woman's sexuality, as a threat. I believe this is what makes Tera Patrick's contribution to society tremendously important. Tera Patrick—as an Asian-American porn star—has shattered what people expected and demanded from Asian-American women. Because of her, we are seen in our entirety. We are seen as whole. Not only our beautiful faces and bodies but the forbidden things that we were not allowed to show, our sexuality and our desire.

Tera, as a businesswoman, also defies the stereotype of the porn star as victim. She owns and runs a global empire that goes way beyond her work as a porn star. She manages so many careers, it's hard to keep up. Porn performer, actress, lingerie designer, talk-show host, producer, director, CEO, etc. She's proof that yes—you can have it all, and then some. Tera Patrick is a true icon of our time, a fantastic example of the power of femininity, sexuality, and intelligence.

I love that she has decided to tell her story in this book, and so honored to be a small part of it. It's a story that needs to be told because I think that the world would be a better place if we could all grow up to be like Tera Patrick.

Prologue

I woke up in the psych ward at St. Vincent's Hospital in Manhattan strapped to my bed, confused, disoriented, scared, and thinking, "How did I get here? What have I done?" What went down in the previous hours started coming back to me piecemeal, but to this day the night remains one big, blurred, fucked-up nightmare. My brain filled in the missing parts of the night with hallucinations; I have visions of being bundled into a straightjacket and taken away in an ambulance. But according to people who were there, it didn't happen that way. That was all in my warped mind. What actually happened might be even worse. The man who loved me and who I loved the most had to duct tape my hands behind my back to stop me from further hurting myself and him. He had to have me committed to a mental ward of a hospital to save my life.

As I scratched and clawed my way through Evan's Brooklyn loft just hours earlier, the only thought in my mind was to end this. I wanted to end my misery and I wanted to end my life. I couldn't handle any of it anymore. But Evan stayed strong because he knew I was worth saving. Evan took my punches, dodged the heavy objects I hurled at him, suffered through my relentless scratching, and he did the one thing he knew to do: stop the madness and get me help.

I don't remember the ride in his Suburban over to the hospital.

I don't remember Dr. Lugo talking Evan through what to do. I don't remember entering the hospital or being checked into the psychiatric ward. I don't remember being strapped to a gurney and the cops questioning Evan about the night's events. I just remember waking up the next morning in lockdown in the place where they keep the most dangerous mental patients. Was I mental? I didn't believe it. My emotions had taken over my thought process, and I was reduced to questioning everything around me and not being able to make sense of any of it.

The psych ward frightened me. I was just a porn chick going through a rough time trying to get out of my contract. Why was I in a room behind locked doors that doctors had to be buzzed in and out of? Why was I in a room with four beds with a variety of women whom I did not relate to, who were not like me? The girl in the bed next to me was a black girl younger than me who had tried to kill herself. She was obsessed with shrimp parmesan and her sister would bring it to her daily, and every day she'd offer me some and each time I'd say no. To this day, the sight of shrimp parmesan sends chills up my spine. I wasn't there to make friends. At first, I wanted nothing to do with the place or anyone in it.

In the bed next to her was a Middle Eastern girl with black curly hair and a flashlight she'd shine around the room after the lights went out. She didn't talk much, but she did mumble her prayers a lot. I would pretend not to hear her. She scared me. I overheard the nurses say that she had delusions about becoming a suicide bomber and that's why she was in the ward. The bed at the end was host to a revolving array of patients whom I don't really remember.

The reality of the night before started coming back to me, and bits and pieces were told to me. I realized that I'd had a major meltdown. A psychotic break. A suicide attempt. I was inconsolable. I was out of my mind. There was no talking me off the ledge this time, as Evan had done before.

I was in St. Vincent's psych ward for fourteen long days, and it was not what you could call time well spent. I just lay there in my hospital bed like a statue. I wanted nothing but out. But I did everything you *shouldn't* do if you want to be released from the psych ward. In full denial for the first few days, I acted out in every way imaginable. I figured if they think I'm crazy, I might as well play the part. I talked to myself out loud. I refused medication. I wouldn't eat anything. I picked fights with other patients. I took it all out on Evan, calling him daily and cursing him out for the entire ward to hear.

I pulled the diva act and tried to own that pay phone. My cell phone had been confiscated, so the pay phone was my only connection to the outside world. So, when anyone else tried to use the phone, I unleashed a shit-storm of anger, screaming, "I'm on the fucking phone! You wait your fucking turn! I'm on the phone! I'll be done when I'm done! I'll fucking kill you!"

Making death threats in the psych ward is not exactly the way to prove that you're not crazy and get released. One day, I even tried to escape. When those buzz-in, locked doors opened, I made a run for it, forcing the orderly to wrestle me to the ground.

When I realized there was no way out unless I played by the rules, I threw the rules in their face. They had been asking me to shower for days and I refused. I was defiant and angry and anti-authority. After days of nagging me to shower, I finally said, "Fuck it. You want me to shower? OK, I'll shower." So I stripped off all of my clothes, walked out of my room into the hallway completely naked, and looked at the first nurse who came my way and said, "OK. You want me to shower? Here I am. Where's the fucking shower?"

As much as this experience was the lowest point of my life, I'm grateful for it. Sometimes you need to go off the rails of the crazy train to get on the right track of your life. And that's exactly what I did.

Sinner Takes All

CHAPTER 1

Idol Worship

How bad do you want what you want? I wanted to be famous and adored so bad it nearly killed me. Well, in all honestly, *I* nearly killed me.

But before we get to that, let me start at the beginning. . . .

In 1986 I was ten years old and my mother had already left us. It was just me, Linda Ann Hopkins, and my dad, David Hopkins, a carefree hippie of English, Dutch, and Irish descent. I was born in Great Falls, Montana, but was living with my dad in Fresno. On a rare father-daughter day out, he took me to a thrift store in town to do some shopping. We were on a budget. As we made our way though the tiny, cramped shop, I saw her hanging on the dusty wall behind some cracked vases and rusty candelabras. It was a beautiful black-and-white photograph of Marilyn Monroe from the Korean USO tour she did in 1954. She was beaming as she posed for hundreds of handsome men in uniform, who in turn were ogling her in all her blond-haired, blue-eyed glory.

Something lit up inside me when I saw that photograph. I thought, "Someday, men are going to look at me that way."

I couldn't stop staring at this photo, thinking how much I wanted to be that girl. The girl everyone adores. The girl whom fame made

The photo that started it all for me

so happy (little did I know what a sad wreck she really was). All I knew about Marilyn at the time was how much I wanted to exude the power that she did. I wanted to be famous like that. I just didn't know what for yet. I never thought it would be for porn.

Around the same time the Marilyn Monroe photo was burned into my brain, I stumbled across another piece of inspiration. I was home alone one day after school. Dad was still at work. I was usually a good girl; I learned manners and respect for others very early on from both of my parents. Although I had never looked through my father's things, on this one day my curiosity got the best of me. I had seen my dad hide a stack of *Playboy* magazines once and was anxious to take a peek inside. I wanted to know what a woman's body looked like. I was just a young girl—an awkward one at that—and I wanted to compare myself to a full-grown woman. It was a natural fascination. The curiosity to see a naked woman left me searching through my dad's teak, tapestry-covered dresser, one of his finds from Thailand when he was there during the Vietnam War. I opened the drawer and there was a *Playboy* with supermodel Paulina Porizkova on the cover. The supermodel and actress was holding back her long, beachy, golden brown hair with a lean, elegant arm and gazing at the camera with her ice blue eyes emanating a fierce self-confidence.

I thought Paulina was the most beautiful woman in the world, and I couldn't stop staring at her photos in *Playboy*. I was even more impressed when I learned she'd married Ric Ocasek, the lead singer of the rock band the Cars. She was a rock wife and a beautiful supermodel, and I just idolized her for that. I wanted what she had. It was that Paulina cover that made me want to be in *Playboy*. From the moment I saw this cover in the summer of 1987, I had a simple quest: be a *Playboy* model, be married to a rock star, and be rich, famous, and adored.

LOOKING UP TO STARS like Marilyn and Paulina was my escape. My parents separated when I was ten. I didn't have my mom or dad to talk to, because they fought a lot and were so wrapped up in themselves. So instead I escaped into a fantasy world of supermodels, celebrity, pin-up girls, *Playboy* Playmates, and rock stars as I flipped through the pages of my dad's issues of *Playboy, Rolling Stone, LIFE*, and whatever music or teen magazine I could get my hands on. I thought about what these gorgeous celebrities would be like in person, what it would be like to live their lives and to be as cool and happy as they seemed to be in the pictures. I would daydream about these models, rock stars, and actresses instead of doing my schoolwork. My grades suffered and I got a lot of notes from the teacher that read "Linda doesn't apply herself enough." Fair enough.

I would also rummage through my father's cassette tapes—he was a rocker—and lust after Jim Morrison. To this day, if I could go back in time and fuck a famous rock star it, would be Jim Morrison. I idolized the Doors, Led Zeppelin, and Pink Floyd—the older bands that my dad was into.

I wouldn't know until years later, after some therapy, that what I was doing was filling the void left by parents who weren't there for me. Some kids in tough situations cope with absent parents by overeating, others with being sexually inappropriate (more on this later), others with drugs and alcohol or getting into trouble at school. For me, at age ten, I disappeared into daydreaming about what it would be like to live the lives of those models, rock stars, and celebrities I read about in magazines or saw on television.

I was a big dreamer; it's all I had at the time. Well, that and my younger sister, Debra, but once my parents split, my sister chose to live with my mother full-time and I chose to live with my father. But Dad wasn't around much. He did the best he could, but he was working all the time and never home. I was home alone a lot and up until about age twelve, I was a very introverted, insecure, and lonely young girl.

I was not popular with the boys, but that was OK because I wasn't into boys then. My sister, the cheerleader and volleyball player, was the popular one in school. I was the dorky jock—running cross-country, reading, and hiking were my loves. I got high marks in physical education, but low to below-average marks in other classes at Fresno's Lincoln Elementary School. My teachers were right—I just didn't apply myself. I'd rather hole up in my bedroom or the library and read a Nancy Drew novel instead of doing my math homework.

On My Bookshelf as a Kid:

Nancy Drew and the Hardy Boys Super Sleuths!, by Carolyn Keene and Franklin W. Dixon

Days with Frog and Toad, by Arnold Lobel

Are You There God? It's Me, Margaret and *Forever,* by Judy Blume

Sweet Valley High #1: Double Love, by Francine Pascal

Ramona Quimby, Age 8, by Beverly Cleary

Helter Skelter: The True Story of the Manson Murders, by Vincent Bugliosi with Curt Gentry

On My Bookshelf Today:

The Encyclopedia of Serial Killers: A Study of the Chilling Criminal Phenomenon, from the "Angels of Death" to the "Zodiac" Killer, by Michael Newton

Marilyn: A Biography, by Norman Mailer

The Sexual Life of Catherine M., by Catherine Millet

The Secret Language of Relationships: Your Complete Personology Guide to Any Relationship with Anyone, by Gary Goldschneider and Joost Elffers

Who Moved My Cheese? by Spencer Johnson, M.D.

Screw the Roses, Send Me the Thorns: The Romance and Sexual Sorcery of Sadomasochism, by Philip Miller and Molly Devon

A People's History of the United States, by Howard Zinn

Playboy: The Complete Centerfolds, by Chronicle Books

Some of my favorite books were considered inappropriate reading for a young girl my age. I would read any book on serial killers that I could get my hands on. I was fascinated with the psychology of murderers. I spent a lot of time during recess in the library reading about John Wayne Gacy and Charles Manson. I was fascinated with Gacy because he would dress up as a clown, and I was really terrified of clowns, so I wanted to know more. I wasn't into the gory details; I was into the "why" of it all. I wanted to know what motivated them. When I would read that their moms were prostitutes or that their parents beat them or that they came from broken homes or were sexually abused, I would look around me and look at the other kids and think, "Are they going to be serial killers?"

Am *I* going to be a serial killer? *I'm* from a broken home and, as you will soon read, *my* mother abused me. I would think, "Can this happen to me?" I was captivated by the thought. I was convinced, and I still am today, that anyone can be a serial killer. I think I could kill somebody if I had to. Well, I did almost kill *myself*, but we'll get to that later.

Some of my friends knew I was fascinated by murder. They'd say, "There's Linda talking about *Helter Skelter* again." But I didn't mind. It made me feel smarter. I might have only gotten C's and some D's in school, but if they tested me on serial killers, I would've been a straight-A student.

I was also an awkward-looking child and stood out from the rest of my classmates. I was a lot, I mean *a lot*, taller and thinner than most of the boys and girls at Lincoln. I was naturally thin and extremely fit because I ran cross-country. "Gangly" would be the best word to describe it, but my classmates had other nicknames for me: Spider and Olive Oyl. Oddly, they never made fun of my unibrow or the crooked part in my hair. (Mom wasn't there to straighten it for me, and Dad wasn't exactly putting bows and ribbons in my hair.)

"Oooh, here comes Linda, the spider," boys and girls would taunt every day after school during cross-country practice out on the track. "Look at Linda, the spider. She's got spider arms. She has spider legs. She's a *Spiderwoman*!"

The thing was, I did kind of look like a spider. I was tall and thin, and my limbs stuck out of the awful mustard-and-red uniforms they made us wear for gym class. The knee socks barely touched my knees, despite me constantly pulling them up as high as they would go.

I don't remember who started the teasing, but everyone certainly joined in, especially Tiffany and Kelly Parisi, twin sisters and head cheerleaders. They were straight out of central casting for pretty, bitchy classmate rivals. They were shorter, with an athletic build; kind of stocky with those thick thigh muscles that dancers or cheerleaders have; and they had short wavy brown hair, making them the complete opposite of lanky me with my long dark straight hair. But they were considered the prettiest girls in school, and we had a mutual hatred for one another.

When they weren't picking on me during cross-country practice, they would nail me in the hallway at school for what I was wearing. Kelly would say, "Oh God, Linda. You're too skinny. *Who* are those jeans by?"

Esprit and Guess were the big brands of the day, but I wasn't exactly a fashionista in grade school like the Parisis, so I wore button-fly dark Levi's from the boys' section of the affordable department store Mervyns. I was more of the hippie girl who didn't care what she looked like or what she wore. I loved Levi's because Dad wore Levi's and Dad was cool, but I also wore them because unlike Guess or Esprit, you could buy Levi's in different lengths, and I needed a few extra inches than most girls and boys.

The twin twits never understood my comebacks because my wit was informed by my fascination with serial killers. "Oh yeah, well your father is a serial killer. Ever wonder why you have that van with no windows? Serial killer van!" I'd say to the Parisi twins.

"*Huh?*" was their usual response.

I never cried or backed down at the teasing. Most of the time I would just let my keychain do the talking for me. I got this keychain from a gumball machine that was in the shape of a hand, and I bent the fingers down so the middle finger was the only one sticking up. It was attached to my cardinal red JanSport backpack, so when I turned my back on them they were sure to see it. It was the most direct way I could find to let them know that I didn't give a fuck.

But I did wonder why I got picked on so much. I didn't realize until many years later when I was all grown up that the bitchy Parisi twins must have been jealous of my height and figure. At the time, I didn't consider my looks at all and I certainly didn't know if I was pretty or ugly. I just knew I was different.

That's why I wanted to look at those nude photos of other women; because I wanted to see how I compared to them. I wanted to see what a beautiful woman was supposed to look like or simply to know what other women looked like.

So when I saw that Paulina Porizkova *Playboy* cover that day in my father's dresser drawer with her long, lean arm framing her face, I thought, Well she's thin and has skinny arms and legs and she's in fucking *Playboy*. I felt more OK with myself after seeing that photo.

Needless to say, I didn't have many friends. But when I did bring friends home, I was embarrassed about how we lived. We had a nice two-bedroom apartment in Fresno, but it was filled with treasures from my father's travels when he was a cook in the Air Force as well as lots of strange things from my mother's homeland of Thailand. When my dad came back to America after being stationed in Thailand during the Vietnam War, he brought back all of these audacious pieces of furniture and accessories. We had green jade elephants and colorful tapestries everywhere and a hideous ceramic rooster that served no purpose but to embarrass me. I was so self-conscious of what my schoolmates thought. And Dad was always cooking up some traditional Thai dish, which filled the small apartment with exotic and pungent smells.

"Oooh, your house smells like fish and you have weird green elephants," is what I figured everyone thought who came into our house. Deep down, I thought my parents' exotic style was cool, but I was also embarrassed by it. Being half Thai, though, didn't embarrass me because so many people in my area of California are of Asian descent. I fit right in on that front.

I think the problem with my parents' relationship was simply that they were too young to be married. My mother—her name is Preeya—was fourteen and only spoke a little bit of English when she met my twenty-year-old father. She was a busgirl on the base in Thailand where Dad was stationed. She was almost eighteen when they got married in Thailand and left for America together. In Thai culture, a girl who moved out of her house without being married was considered a whore. So she was anxious to get married to move out from under her parents' control. Dad and she were good friends, and it seemed like a good idea at the time.

But the marriage wasn't all it was cracked up to be and she became angrier and unhappier, and this increased greatly as I turned eight, nine, and ten years old. My dad was gone a lot because he was working and going to college. He's had many occupations over the years. He was a U.S. Forest Ranger, a truck driver, a pot grower, a teacher, and a winemaker. (He's had a steady job since I was twenty-five, though, as head winemaker for Bridlewood Winery in San Ynez, California.) My mom had a tough time assimilating to American culture. She took ESL classes at night and took care of my sister and me by herself during the day, and she soon started working as a nurse. I try to put myself in my parents' shoes. Here's my dad just wanting the perfect little Asian wife, and there's my mom, trapped in a house with two kids, barely speaking English, and her husband is never around. I think she resented having kids at such a young age. And my dad wasn't coming home some nights, so that wasn't helping their relationship. Then Mom started to not come home at night. She was rebelling against him. So I had neither parent around. When they were home together, the arguing was intense. I'd sit up in bed at night and hear them scream at each other and think, "Why don't you get divorced already?"

That wasn't the only problem. There was also my mother's violent temper. I desperately wished I could have told my father what my mother was doing to me on those nights she was home and he wasn't. She was this petite, but strong, karate-chopping type of woman who would take out her frustrations on me with anything she could get her hands on. She'd whack me with a broom, throw a shoe at me, or just backhand me across the face. I think she took it out on me more than my sister because I was closer to my father at the time and she didn't like that.

I was Daddy's little girl for most of grade school. We'd go hiking, camping, fishing, and even hunting together. Well, *he* hunted; I picked flowers. We were very outdoorsy and earthy. We even had a pet pig when I was younger. But what Dad and I really bonded over was music. We listened to music together and watched music movies like Led Zeppelin's *The Song Remains the Same*. He was high as a kite, saying to me, "Linda! Linda! Come here. You have to see Jimmy Page play the guitar with a bow." I didn't know who or what he was talking about and I didn't care that he was stoned; all I knew was that Dad was paying attention to me and I loved what he was showing me. I loved the raw energy of rock stars. I loved the shirtless Jimmy Page. I loved it all.

Mom and I were not close. Her unhappiness and anger made a barrier around her. I felt displaced in my own family and alone. From around age seven or eight, I had to rely on myself—cook my own meals, do my own laundry, get myself ready for school, etc. In a way, it was good because I learned to be self-reliant and very independent, which I still am today. But as a child, you want both of your parents to help you with the simple things and participate in your life.

From one of my camping trips with Dad

The worst fight I had with my mother was the day she snapped. After my parents finally parted ways in 1986, I was staying with my mother on weekends and with my father during the week. It was a Saturday afternoon at her apartment in Fresno, and I made a comment about wanting to be back at my dad's house. I think I said something like, "Fuck you, I want to live with Dad all the time." Little did I know how tough it was for her at the time to not have custody and how betrayed she felt when I chose my father over her. She was going through a really rough time. She was working two jobs, didn't have family around, lived paycheck-to-paycheck, and didn't even have an emotional support system after the divorce.

So we were arguing. She usually argued in Thai and spoke it really fast so I couldn't understand what she was saying anyway. She grabbed me by the hair and then punched me straight in the face. I held my face in pain and looked at her with such hatred and shock. I felt so confused and devastated by that one blow. This is my

My mom

mother, the one person who is supposed to protect me and instead she is hurting me. She then wrapped her hands around my throat and began choking me. I was a strong-willed kid, and I was not going down without a fight. That's not me. I did my best to fight back, but she was a lot stronger than me. She was a small Thai woman but the devil inside her gave her this superhuman strength. The fight went on for at least a half hour.

"No! No! Don't hurt her!" my eight-year-old sister, Debby, cried and screamed at my mother from across the room.

Mom hit me again. She was hitting me like she was fighting off some sort of attacker. I was beaten and bruised and my hair was in matted clumps from where she grabbed it. And the fight would've kept going had my dad not walked in to pick me up at the exact moment her fingers were clenching my throat. He had to put his body between my mom and me and reach out his arms to stop the brawling.

"Dad, I swear I never want to see her again!" I screamed with tears running down my swollen face.

"OK. You don't have to," he said.

I lived with Dad full-time after that. And I didn't speak to my mother again until five years later, when my world came crashing down for a second time.

That one fight changed my relationship with my mother and with women in general forever. I wasn't mature enough at the time to realize that my mom was the way she was because she was abused as a child herself. I shut down emotionally and closed myself off, especially to women. But men, that was a different story. This series of events made my Lolita ways kick in a bit. I think that's why from a young age I dreamed of marrying a really great man, a man I could feel secure with. But at the time it led to a pattern where every time I was hurt, I went to a man. Any man.

Sixth grade: my first laser photo

Chapter 2

The Switch

I clearly remember my first orgasm. I was twelve. I wasn't a sexual child until I met Mark. He was the uncle of my friend Danielle. He was twenty-five, about five foot seven, skinny and lanky, with short brown hair. He kind of looked like Scott Weiland from Stone Temple Pilots. He rode a Harley-Davidson motorcycle and worked at the gas station down the street. I knew he was way older than me, but that didn't stop the huge crush I had on him. He was my first of many motorcycle-men crushes.

I was walking to school one day, carrying my books, and he pulled out of the gas station on his bike and just the sight of him excited me. I dropped my books and stared at him. I think it was the first orgasm I ever felt. It was at least the first tingling I ever had down there in that way. And I had not had any sexual feeling like that before, at least not that I remember. I vividly recall this intense sexual tingling and getting wet in my panties. I had thoughts of him for days after that and finally one day I made out with him.

I would see Mark often at Danielle's house (she lived with him and her mom in a Santa Rosa apartment) and couldn't help but flirt with him. He noticed the way I looked at him, smiled at him, and hung on his every word. I liked making a man pay attention to me, because I wasn't getting a lot of attention at home. I didn't think of the age difference at all. When you're young, sexually curious, and starving for attention, you don't think of those things. Today when I think about it, I see it as twisted and wrong. But in the moment, it was just exciting to have this flirtation with this older man. One day he invited me to come over and look at his books because I was still quite the bookworm at the time. Of course, I went. I loved books and I was flattered by the invitation. I thought it was a great opportunity to flirt more with this cool guy. As I was busy thumbing through his copies of *Easy Rider* magazine and various mechanical motorcycle books, my friend Danielle was busy in another room. Mark and I were sitting close on his living room couch and I kept looking at him with the sultriest look I could muster up for a twelve-year-old. He was flirting with me, too. Our smiles told it all. Each time we'd look at each other, we'd grin from ear to ear. The attraction was obvious, and well, I made it hard to go unnoticed because I was wearing a tight tank top and short-shorts. As we talked closely, we could feel the warmth of each other's breath and the electricity in the air. We couldn't take it anymore, and he finally leaned in and kissed me.

I didn't know how to kiss, but I was going at it like crazy and clinging on to him, holding on to him, and moving my tongue all around his mouth. It was my first French kiss. More than the kissing or the age difference, the thing I remember the most was not wanting to let go of him. I was wrapped in his arms and clutching on to him. It felt so good to be in the arms of a man who liked me.

My friend Danielle walked in on us and said, "You might want to close the blinds." We stopped the make-out session, pulled apart from each other, and I said my good-byes. When I look back on it now, I'm glad Danielle caught us. I think it spooked Mark. I don't know if he would've tried to take it further than kissing, but if Danielle didn't interrupt us, maybe he would've. I don't think I was prepared to handle what could've happened on that couch that day. I'm glad we kissed, but I wasn't ready for anything more. However, in that moment, in that twelve-year-old brain, I probably wouldn't have had the maturity to know that it would've been a bad thing. I think Danielle's interruption might just have saved me from doing something that would've left me with some severe emotional repercussions and a lot of regret down the road.

I also started to *emotionally* cling to men from age twelve. I would befriend the older men in our apartment building. I wasn't sexual with them, and no one ever stepped out of line with me. Unlike so many porn stars, I was never sexually abused or raped. But the men in our building knew I liked to read, and I was a young cute girl with big boobs, and they'd invite me to come over and see their books or to just read at their apartments. I loved the attention. And I guess they liked having a young, hot girl with big tits hanging around their apartment. Even though I was only twelve, I felt like a woman. I learned that having boobs at this young age was very powerful. I saw how men looked at me, and I started to harness that power for my own good. I'd flirt more and would prance around in wifebeaters with no bra, and it would get me what I wanted—like rides to the mall or to rock concerts or escape from boredom and loneliness.

I was obsessed with going to rock concerts in the '80s with my best friend Ally Graham. Her favorite band was Mötley Crüe and mine was Def Leppard. I looked like such a rock slut during those years. I was such an exhibitionist. I would dress in ripped-up jeans with a hole in the butt and only wear concert shirts—cut up, tied up, or off my shoulder. I was a total rock chick, and a big tease at this age. I drooled over every boy with long hair or who rode a bike and looked tough. I wasn't just a rock chick. I was a metal-head. My first concert was Iron Maiden and Saxon, and it left quite a mark on me. I was hooked on going to rock shows from that first concert.

The whole experience was so hot to me, and I started fantasizing more about marrying a music man. I was the girl in love with every lead singer of hot metal bands out there. And I was the girl who was flashing her boobs to Gene Simmons at a Kiss/Slaughter/Winger show, and I know he saw me. I made it hard to be missed.

Officially boy crazy now, it was time for "the talk." With Mom not around, that task was left to my dad. It was not pretty. He said, "I know you're blossoming now and men are going to want to touch you and feel you, but you don't have to do it." That's all he said. That was "the talk." I just said, "OK, Dad." But deep down I was embarrassed for him and it made me kind of sad. If he only knew that it was *me* who wanted to do stuff to the guys, he'd feel horrible. My dad had no idea how much of a tease I was becoming and how at the young age of twelve, I was flirting with older men, kissing lots of boys, and using my sexuality to get what I wanted.

But he did know the effect I had on men and that I was turning into an attractive girl. I was five foot seven with a 34-C chest and twenty-two-inch waist by the time I became a teenager. We spent every weekend in San Francisco because I was attending the Barbizon School of Modeling there—I wanted to be a model so badly.

Me in eighth grade

It didn't take much convincing to get my dad to enroll me in modeling school. He knew how much I wanted to be a model. But more important, I think the reason my dad agreed so readily was because I didn't have a mom in my life to be show me how to become a lady. Modeling school is not just about posing for photos or learning how to put your hair in a pretty bun or how to blend your eye shadow. It was also about how to grow from a girl into a woman, how to be poised and proper and how to present yourself in the best way. I didn't have a mother to teach me those things, and I think he felt bad about that and saw Barbizon as an opportunity for me to have a girlie outlet. It was a positive, healthy extracurricular activity, too, just like taking up sports or ballet. And it gave me something to do. It occupied my time so he didn't have to worry about figuring out what to do with me all the time. Being a single dad to girls can't be easy.

I think the cost was about $90 a week at the time, which was kind of a lot and especially for a single parent. But he worked two jobs and found a way to afford it. He was good at giving me what I wanted within reason. I mean, I didn't have new clothes all the time, and we scrimped on other things, but this was one cost he was willing to pay because he thought it would be good for me.

One day in 1990—I was thirteen years old and in eighth grade—we went to Fisherman's Wharf, where all the tourists in San Francisco go to see the sea lions. And this guy, who had been kind of checking me out, came up to my father and started talking to him. I just assumed it was another creepy old man staring at my tits.

"Your daughter is really beautiful. She's really tall, really thin, and has a great look. Has she ever considered modeling?" the man said to my father.

"Well, I have her enrolled in Barbizon. She wants to be a model," my father cautiously replied.

Meanwhile, I was being very quiet but exploding inside with excitement. I trusted my father to do what was best for me and he did.

"I think she would be a really great model," the man said. "Her look is very contemporary, and I think she could make a lot of money. Why don't you let me do a test shoot with her? I'll send it off and we'll see if anybody bites." He turned out to be a talent scout from Japan named John Teo. A test shoot is like a trial run of a photo shoot. They take photos of you, send them to agencies and pitch you for modeling jobs.

My dad agreed, and the two exchanged numbers. And the following weekend, that's exactly what we did. I had my very first test shoot.

My father's girlfriend at the time, Lori Meyer, came with me. I was very close to her. She was like a mother to me. We would watch *House of Style* with Cindy Crawford on MTV and I would study Cindy's moves to learn how to model. So Lori chaperoned this test shoot, which was at a beach and in a park in San Francisco. All I could think was, "I'm on my way to doing what my idols Marilyn Monroe and Paulina Porizkova do!"

The second John Teo started shooting me in the sand on that beach in a wholesome white top and cutoff jean shorts, I was hooked. I knew this was what I was meant to do. John didn't give me a lot of direction, because I was naturally doing what he needed. I wasn't perfect, but I was pretty relaxed and easy. It was so fun to move to the camera. I was really excited and happy, and it felt right. Lori kept cheering me on, "You're doing great. Turn to the right, stick your hips out, smile!" I was having so much fun. I had to tone down my antics because the shoot was for Japanese scouts and John kept reminding me, "Now remember, this is for Japan and they like their girls to be very ladylike and demure, so don't over-pose."

He also told me not to tan my skin, because the Japanese like their girls to have light pale skin. That was tough for me because besides having natural brown skin from my Thai mother, I was also a sun goddess who would catch rays with baby oil, Hawaiian Tropic, or Ban de Soleil over my skin like I was a basting turkey!

After the shoot, I really had no idea what was going to happen. The whole thing seemed like a lark to me, but I was so excited that my dream of becoming a model might actually come true. John told us the pictures came out great and he went ahead and sent them to different modeling agencies all over the world: Paris, New York, Milan, and Tokyo.

The biggest response came from Tokyo. They were so interested that they sent scouts to come see my dad in Napa Valley, where we were living at the time. They were surprised that I hadn't modeled before and told my dad they wanted to take me back to Tokyo with them. A few weeks later, I signed with the Morning Sun modeling agency in Tokyo, signed with a model manager named Myuki, and was booked to move to Tokyo by myself.

Sure, Dad was hesitant at first. After spending a lot of time apart when Debby and I were younger, Dad and I were finally spending some time together. But I was open to the idea, and eventually so was he, especially after the scout told him that the runway and photo work in Tokyo would easily pay for my college tuition. He knew how much I wanted to model and how much I was enjoying my time at Barbizon, so he saw it as a great opportunity for me. And he did his homework. The agency went through Barbizon. It wasn't just some random, unknown company swooping in to send me off. Barbizon vouched for the company and the agency and helped ease any fears my father might have had. And he trusted me. I don't think the thought crossed his mind that I would get into trouble over there.

In my mind, I was off to be a supermodel and take over the world. In my dad's mind, he was losing his daughter, but gaining college money for me. Dad dropped me off at the airport and said, "This is your big chance. Make the best of it, and call me if you have any issues and I will come there."

Thirteen and a half hours later, I stepped off the plane and there I was in my new home, Tokyo, Japan. I was fourteen years old. And I felt powerful.

I was so young, but it was a very adult experience. I lived in a huge apartment with Joe, the owner of Morning Sun, but he was never around. I had a full-time tutor for school and another tutor to teach me Japanese, which I didn't exactly pick up very well. Luckily, most people in the industry spoke English. We lived in the Omotesandō area of Tokyo, which was a trendy neighborhood. He

Me at age fourteen

had one half of the apartment. I had the other. I was pretty much on my own. When I wasn't at a casting call or booked for a modeling job, I'd spend hours shopping in the market and going into fashion boutiques, blowing my $500 weekly allowance on nonessentials like lip gloss and trendy shoes. Five hundred dollars is not a lot of spending money when you consider the fact that two oranges cost $9 in Tokyo markets at that time.

I was able to make friends right away with a lot of the other girls who worked at the agency. Most of them were much older, in their twenties. It was quite an experience, running around in a foreign country with all these models from all over the world. They were adults and I was a young kid. Even the few girls who were near my age seemed more worldly than me because they had already been in the business a few years. The ones who were sixteen had started when they were twelve. They already knew the ropes, but I didn't.

My best friend among the models was Thea Kulick. She became my big sister. She was British, tall, and very beautiful, with short blond hair and a tight body. She reminded me then of Annie Lennox and now of model Agyness Deyn. I would follow her around and mimic everything that she did. She was very smart and well spoken and I loved her posh English accent. I think part of the reason that I felt so comfortable around her is because my dad's family is English. I had spent some time in England with family, and I really gravitated to Thea.

I loved my new friends, and I was happy when they were around. But when we'd go our separate ways at the end of the day, I'd get really lonely by myself. Nighttime would roll around, and I would be alone in my empty apartment in Tokyo thinking about what my family and friends were doing back home. It was an odd feeling to be so excited to be living out my dream in this exotic place, but at the same time miss the comforts of home, like my dad's cooking or my sister being there to gossip with. It didn't help matters that I was having a hard time trying to learn my way around Tokyo. I had a tutor who was teaching me Japanese every day, but I was failing miserably. But just when I was feeling my lowest, I'd remember that it was still daytime in America. I would pick up the phone and call somebody, anybody, but usually my sister Debby or my best friend, Ally. My phone bill averaged more than $2,500 a month—money that was supposed to go to my college fund. And I would tell Debby and Ally all about whatever was happening. They were particularly interested in my experiences in the clubs in Tokyo because they had never been to a club at all, let alone one in Tokyo. And I was going out every night.

My favorite club was the Lexington Queen in Roppongi, which is where all the rock stars would hang out. We would use our zed cards to get in. A zed card is a modeling calling card. On the front, there was a head shot, and then on the back there were four or five small pictures of you in different modeling poses. They were supposed to be for your cattle calls. And they called them cattle calls because they would literally pile all the models in a van like cattle and take us from booking to booking. If you got booked for a job, you would go back and do it the next day. But when you weren't working, you just kept getting sent out on cattle calls. The door guys at the clubs knew about the zed cards and when they saw one, they would just let you go on in. Models are good for business.

And since we were all models, we would get everything for free: free admission, free food, and free champagne. A lot of the models smoked pot and took pills, especially Valium, and I did too. I had smoked pot for the first time right before I left for Tokyo. My dad's always grown marijuana and has been a big pot smoker, and back in the U.S. I'd stolen some pot out of his hiking backpack and

*One of my headshots
from Japan*

smoked it out of his pipe. It kind of hurt, but I liked the way it
made me feel. I had to lay off smoking when I got to Tokyo because
I was having a little too much fun. I would go over to friends'
houses to listen to music and drink a little bit of champagne.
We would smoke a joint and the next thing I knew it was four in
the morning and I would realize, "I've got to be up at seven in the
morning and I look like shit!"

But even totally sober, I was very outgoing—a stark contrast to
my early childhood years. I was the first one to introduce myself
and the first to volunteer for karaoke, which was, of course, a huge
thing in Japan. This was the beginning of feeling good about myself
and not being the shy girl who dreamed of being wanted. Instead,
I was coming out of my shell and into my sexuality and loving it. I
finally got out of my rut and into another environment and found
a place where people found me sexy. No one was calling me Spider
in Tokyo. I was really feeling the power of my sexuality and the
power of being attractive to the opposite sex.

I was also always the girl with the shortest skirt and the tallest
thigh-high books. I loved showing off my legs. And I would typi-

cally wear a lacy bra with a little sheer top tied over it. A couple of the girls in the group were a little jealous of me, I think. They would bitchily say to me, "With that long hair and those boobs, you're not going to get a lot of work." But I was working every day. My first job was a runway show. I also did a lot of work for cosmetics companies, including Shiseido, and for the jean company Gerivobe. Often, I'd be hired to model makeup at the cosmetics counter in department stores as well.

I was living the life. Nothing turned me on more than turning it on for the camera, and sometimes photographers were there to benefit from that. I lost my virginity to a thirtysomething photographer on one of my earliest shoots in Tokyo in my first year there. I can't remember his name, but I'll never forget this shoot. He was really, really hot. He had gorgeous, thick, short brown hair. His frame was small, his waist thin, and his body was all lithe muscle like David Beckham. He could have been a model himself when he was younger, but his face was a bit menacing-looking. I think I was attracted to him because he looked like a bad boy, and I loved a bad boy—musicians, motorcycle men, model photographers.

He took charge and he told me I was beautiful. I loved posing for him, and seeing how he wanted me. I wanted him, too. We were flirting a bit before we started shooting, and when he'd touch me to move my hair out of the way or fix the strap of my top, my skin felt hot. I was so excited to be working with him.

He was feeding me champagne and Valium and I was getting wasted. I'd had plenty of drinks before, both in the clubs in Japan and at the winery my dad worked at in California, but I was a different kind of drunk on this occasion. It was the kind of drunk where your head falls back but your eyes stay staring out in front of you, the kind of drunk where you're not really sure what's happening, the kind of drunk where you lose your virginity to a man twice your age. Yeah, the kind of drunk where statutory rape happens.

"You look so beautiful," he'd say. "Move your hair to the side. Perfect." His direction turned me on. I wanted to feel like a sexy woman, not a fourteen-year-old kid straight off the plane from California, and the way he told me how to look like a grown woman turned me on wildly.

The shoot was going great and we were flirting with each other, and then he kissed me. I felt warm, fuzzy, and very soft. And most of all, I felt wanted. I felt desired. He made me feel like my dream of becoming Paulina Porizkova was coming true. Right then. Right there in his photo studio. He made me feel how I felt looking at Paulina's photo that first time in my dad's *Playboy*.

I was posing on a chaise lounge in this little dress and he found every excuse to get closer to me, to remove the space between his camera and my body. He'd say, "Let me pull your strap up." Or, "Here, it would look better if you unbuttoned one more button." The next thing I knew, he slid his hand up my thigh and I shivered.

I'll never forget the feeling I got in the pit of my stomach. I still get that feeling sometimes even today. It's a feeling that something is just not right and I can't quite put my finger on it. It almost takes my breath away. I had that feeling when he started feeling up my leg and putting his fingers inside me, and touching my nipples. I was very turned on and hot for him, but something didn't feel right.

Finally, he lay on top of me, lifted up my dress, pulled my panties off, and spread apart my drunken legs. I was having an out-of-body experience. He finally inserted himself, and I was wet for him. We had sex for about fifteen minutes, and I remember being wasted during most of it. But I also remember feeling some pain. I was a virgin, after all. I just kept thinking, "Is this what it's supposed to feel like?!" It felt feverish. He was like a jackhammer, and I was not enjoying it.

I never said "no" or "stop." I felt like it was my fault because I enticed him. I brought it on. I flirted with him and kissed him. I had this way of flirting too far, where you push and push and push and tease and tease and tease until something finally happens. That's what this was. Later on, I didn't talk to the other models or my manager about it because I didn't want to get a reputation or lose jobs, so I just kept quiet. To me, at the time, it wasn't rape because I consented. But it wasn't right, either. I always thought I'd lose my virginity to someone like Joe Elliott, the lead singer of Def Leppard, in a field of flowers. This was not that.

After we were done, I told him I was a virgin, and he asked, "Are you kidding?"

"Nope. I am."

"Wow, maybe I should have been gentler."

"Why?"

"Well, you don't treat a virgin the same way you treat any old regular girl."

After that, we continued the photo shoot as if nothing happened. This is where "The Switch" kicked in. This is when I changed forever and it sent me on the path to porn. He was done. I was done. OK, I can move on and finish the shoot now. I was completely professional and acted like nothing had happened. I had a job to do and I was going to do it well. This switch kicked in where I could turn it on and turn it off at will. I could go through a painful, weird, drunken sexual experience and in the next second be back in front of the camera all smiles and ready to give it my all again. Have sex, move on. This MO would serve me quite well when I starting doing porn.

I actually liked turning this sex queen on and off. It really did work well for me for a while, and not just in porn, but also in my real-life relationships. If that first sexual experience went differently, would I still be a porn star? I don't know. I think my emotional life would've been different, that's for sure. But I don't have any regrets, because if I wasn't a famous porn star, I wouldn't have been able to call up the man of my dreams from three thousand miles away and make him my husband. I wouldn't have millions of dollars and be recognized all over the world. As fucked-up as it may sound, if it weren't for porn, I probably would still be this shy little introverted girl nicknamed Spider. As violating as it may seem, that sexual experience made me who I am today, and I love who I am today.

Two days after losing my virginity, I wanted to have sex again. I went out with a group of models—Alberto and Nancy from Holland, Cole from Florida, Kay from L.A. (who was dating Guns N' Roses bassist Duff McKagan), and Orly and Galit from Israel. We headed out to the Lexington Queen and I finally came face to face with one of my idols: Axl Rose of Guns N' Roses. The band was in town to play the Tokyo Dome, and I couldn't go to the show because I had a job, but we were all going to meet up after.

I was sitting there on one of the couches, glass of champagne in hand, strobe lights pulsating away to the club music playing loudly. Over the music, I said to one of the other girls, "Oh, my God. This is so cool! We're going to meet Guns N' Roses." And just as the words left my mouth, Axl Rose came walking through the club in a long fur coat. I was so starstruck that I didn't speak to him. I didn't say anything. I just stared at everything around me. I was so intimidated being around this crowd of people, but I was also keenly aware of how cool it was to be so young and in a foreign country and among all these beautiful, famous people. I knew that I was now closer than ever to fucking a rock star.

I was pretty sexed-up this particular night. I spent much of the evening chatting up some Guns N' Roses groupies who were much older and more experienced than I was. With a few drinks in me I felt loosened up enough to ask a question that was on my mind: How do you give a blowjob? I was already plotting the end of my night and I knew I wanted to fool around with someone, so I thought I should learn a few tricks, and who better to learn from than these gorgeous rocker-chick groupies. A really hot petite blond groupie gave me the best advice of my sexual life up to this point:

"Here's what you do—practice on a popsicle. Get your mouth nice and wet and start by opening up wide and putting your lips out over the popsicle, then slowly slide the popsicle as far down your throat as you can go while making a sucking motion with your mouth. Alternate between sucking hard and fast and teasing it slowly with the tip of your tongue. Whatever you do, don't do the same motion the entire time. You have to change it up!"

Instead of going home with one of the guys in the band, though, I went home with two models, Alberto and Cole. Alberto was tall and skinny with thick black wavy hair and a black beard he kept neatly trimmed. He had a really sharp nose and square jaw and piercing ice blue eyes. Like many models, he was a chain smoker, and I found it sexy. Cole had thick brown wavy hair and had more of a husky, football-player build with a great broad chest.

They got me drunk on a drink called Cookies & Cream, which was a sickly sweet concoction containing lots of Bailey's Irish Cream.

I was feeling like a sex kitten and it made me feel in control. I wanted to wrap my arms and legs around every hot guy I saw and just rub my body on them. I just loved men and even though that first experience wasn't great, I wanted sex again. It made me feel powerful. It still does. So the guys took me back to their apartment in Tokyo and I couldn't wait to put the Guns N' Roses' groupies' advice to use. There was no time to practice on a popsicle; the real deal was happening right then and there. I remember putting Alberto's dick in my mouth for the first time and being excited to drive him crazy. The groupie girl's words echoed in my head: "Whatever you do, don't do the same motion the entire time." With that in mind, I was all over his cock. I went from taking it deep in my throat to flicking the head with my tongue to sucking him hard and fast to taking his hard cock in and out of my mouth as he begged for more. It was easy because he didn't have a big dick, so I was able to really go to town on it. I'm sure it was the worst blowjob ever, but he seemed to like it. We had sex after that while Cole jerked off and watched.

At the time, I couldn't figure out why I was doing what I was doing. I was so immature. Just a little kid. All the other girl models were like, "What the fuck is her problem?" I think it was obvious to everyone that I was drinking and slutting around more than the other girls, especially girls my age. It wasn't that bad, though. I only slept with two guys. But I fooled around with three others. For a girl my age it was a little out of control.

A week later, I couldn't sleep and Galit gave me Valium. I'd taken it before, but taking it this time set me on a bad path. At first I took it just to sleep, but pretty soon I was taking it all the time.

I was fourteen years old, living on my own in a foreign country, and sleeping with guys twice my age. How much could a few pills hurt?

CHAPTER 3

The Party's Over

When I wasn't working, I would take a handful of Valium, pass out, not eat for two days, and aimlessly walk around Tokyo spending the majority of the money I was supposed to save for college. I was earning money hand over fist every week and would blow it on expensive designer clothes (and lots of boots) at ritzy boutiques in town. Looking back, maybe they shouldn't have paid a young girl directly. Maybe it should've gone through my dad so he could put more away for college and just give me what I needed to live on.

I took Valium every day and I was full-on addicted. I took it mostly so that I could sleep, but I was *always* sleeping, up to twelve hours a day. And I wasn't exactly Sleeping Beauty. I was looking pale and thin. My hair was falling out and my nails were getting brittle. I wasn't going to castings because I'd oversleep. And when I did get up in time, I would look like such shit that I'd end up blowing off a job.

I was a not-so-beautiful mess. From ages fourteen to sixteen, I was living in Tokyo by myself with no structure, no family, no rules, and lots of money. It's what I thought I wanted, but it was lonely. I was really missing home. Some days I was on top of the world and

I was so happy to shoot and work. And other days, I couldn't drag myself out of bed. I didn't understand what was going on with me. I didn't realize that I needed help, because no one was there to tell me. I was on my own.

I was calling my best friend back home, Ally, and my sister a lot. But my sister was younger than me and Ally was my age, so they didn't exactly have any words of wisdom for me. Besides, they were wrapped up in their own lives. Life was going on without me, and it was starting to get to me.

My worst night was the night Ally told me she lost her virginity. "Who did you do it with?" I anxiously asked her.

"Seth," she replied.

Seth?! I was shocked.

Seth was a guy who'd had a crush on *me* before I left for Tokyo. We were actually kind of boyfriend/girlfriend. And when I left, he moved on to her. It hurt badly. I was jealous. Because she lost her virginity to a guy she really liked and my first time was shitty.

I didn't have a mother or even a mother figure to help me deal with these new feelings and emotions. So, I did the only thing I knew would make me feel good: I took three Valium, went to bed, and cried and cried and cried. Sometimes I'd sleep for twenty-four hours straight.

The days were getting rougher. I was becoming more of a mess. I had no friends anymore. The models I had befriended now thought of me as this stupid little drug-addled slut. Mean, but true.

I knew my dream was crashing down on me, but I was ready to go home anyway. I was so tired of being sick all day from the pills and champagne. Work stopped coming my way. I wanted to get away from the guys I'd had sex with. I didn't save nearly as much for college as I had planned or my father had hoped for. I was ready to leave, but not brave enough to do it. The decision ended up being my dad's. He caught wind of what my life was like in Tokyo and called up my agency and warned, "She's underage. She's drinking. *You're* going to get in trouble for this. And I know she's having sex. She's only sixteen." I know I spilled to my sister Debby that I'd had sex and it was supposed to be our little secret, but then she went and told my dad. I felt so betrayed. Next thing I knew I was on a plane back to America, my dreams of becoming a famous supermodel gone forever.

CHAPTER 4

Homecoming Scream

I was sixteen years old and already a washed-up model. Lovely. My father was so pissed that he didn't even pick me up at San Francisco Airport when I returned home from Tokyo. My agent, Yumi, picked me up instead, and I detoxed from the Valium at her house. A few days later, I had to face my father.

He sat me down for a serious talk. "What do you want to do when you grow up?" he asked.

"I want to be a fucking model!" I cried.

"Well, you had two years to do that and you fucked it up. It's time to grow up and be part of the real world," he replied sternly, very fatherly.

"Fuck you" was all I could say. I was pissed too. Pissed that I wasted this great opportunity. Pissed that I was forced to come home. Pissed that deep down I actually missed home and brought this on myself. Pissed that I disappointed my father. Pissed at my father for making me come home. I was so pissed, in fact, that I asked to stay with my mother in Merced, California, near Modesto. Yes, the mother I hadn't talked to or seen since our horrible fight when I was ten.

Living with my mother again was hell. Nothing had changed.

We fought every day. She wasn't happy that I was smoking and making friends with older people in the building. Every time she'd get mad at me, she'd throw my failed modeling career in my face. "Oh, well, the *supermodel* doesn't like it. What's the *supermodel* going to do about it?" she'd say. It went on for six months until we finally had it out in her Hyundai on the way to the mall when she called me a "crazy chain-smoking supermodel bitch." I called my father and gave in. "OK. I'm ready to be normal and come home." I didn't talk to my mother for another sixteen years after that.

But this time, it wasn't because she beat me. I was just being a rebellious teenager and figured if Mom wouldn't let me live the way I wanted, I'd go to Dad's. I was playing both sides. I didn't realize I was hurting her or abandoning her. Like many sixteen-year-olds, I hated my mother. And I never worked through the reality of her beating me when I was a child. I just buried those feelings and pretended like it never happened. At that age, you don't have the emotional maturity to work it out or the wisdom to know that I should've let her be a mom and guide me. Instead, I took the easier way out and just left and never dealt with it. At the time, I didn't know how to handle my feelings or confront my problems. I just knew how to move on. Besides, she was condescending and mean and I just didn't want to deal with it anymore. So, back to Dad's I went.

When I showed up on Dad's doorstep in Gresham, Oregon, where he was teaching horticulture at Gresham College, he looked at me and said, "Welcome home. I love you. You're going to college."

One thing I liked about being back home with Dad was his girlfriend, and my soon-to-be new stepmom, Kara. She was only about ten years older than me and I thought she was really cool, hip, and pretty. We got along great. I craved a female relationship. I craved a mother. She was like a cool big sister and a mother all in one. She liked the same music as me; she'd take me shopping and even taught me how to drive a stick shift. And I could easily talk to her about my problems. And she brought youthfulness to my father, which I was grateful for. I didn't want him to end up with some cranky old lady. I was happy he found a younger woman who could make him happy and feel young again.

It was in Oregon that I learned how to fuck. Sure, I was experienced by then, but I didn't really know what I was doing until I met Paul when I was sixteen. Paul was twenty years old with long, straight blond hair, muscles, and a demon tattoo on his shoulder blade. And he drove a badass lime green Barracuda muscle car and worked out a lot. That combination spelled instant love for me.

If it weren't for Paul, I'd probably be a bad lay today. With him, I finally enjoyed sex for the first time. I was so in love with Paul that it made the sex all the better. We did it every day. He taught me how to fuck, how to have an orgasm, and how to master my blow-job technique. I used the blowjob tips I got from the Guns N' Roses groupies in Tokyo, but Paul was really the one who helped me take my BJ to the next level. He showed me the trick where you give a hand job while you are sucking and once the dick is all wet and slobbery, you twist your hand around the head of the penis after you come up the shaft. Paul also taught me how to be dirty and introduced me to sucking balls.

The first time we had sex was the first time I ever had sex on top, and it changed everything for me. It's truly best when you're on top. He flipped me up on top of him and rubbed my clit with his thumb and bit my nipples and I just kept coming and coming. He had me at that fuck. He was doing everything he could to please me. I was hooked on him instantly.

With my teenage hormones raging, I told my father, "Dad, I'm in love with Paul and I want to be with him." He must have thought, "What do you know about love, little girl?" That night, my dad and my new stepmom went out and I was left alone in the apartment in Gresham. I packed a bag and left for Paul's place. I found out later that when he returned home, he shut the door to my room and cried. I put my dad through so much.

At age eighteen

But I was in love. Really in love. And I was having fun. Paul's parents paid our rent. We were total bums. I'd drink champagne all day and he'd drink beer. And we'd fuck. He would touch me and I would instantly crave him. It was magnetic. He made me go crazy. I was finally having sex that I really, really enjoyed and I didn't want it to stop. I wanted it every day, every way.

Paul treated me great, but he was very jealous and that ended up doing us in. He would take me to rock concerts and I would fantasize about having sex with Paul *and* the lead singer of whatever band was playing, so one day I asked Paul for a threesome. He said no. I wanted a threesome so badly, but he was just too jealous to deal. The fantasy of having sex with two guys turned me on more than anything else, and it was driving me crazy that I couldn't have it. If a guy even looked at me, Paul would be like, "What the fuck are you looking at?"

Our relationship ended when I was eighteen and I couldn't control my raging hormones anymore. I really wanted to fuck the singer in this local band named Terry. So, I did. He was a total scumbag with long straight hair he'd wear in a ponytail, and he wore a dirty leather jacket. I was bored. I'd been with Paul for two years and I was getting restless. Paul wasn't letting me act on any of my sexual fantasies, and frankly, I just craved a different cock. So I cheated on Paul with Terry and Paul flipped out and kicked my cheating ass out the door.

"Get the fuck out of my house, you fucking slut!" he said.

In a fit of jealous rage, he ripped the blinds off the kitchen windows and punched holes in the wall. I thought he was going to beat the fuck out me, but he didn't. He just made me feel horrible about how I'd hurt him.

"I can't believe you did this!" he yelled. "That guy is a fucking scumbag."

I was still basking in the glow of fucking that fucking scumbag. All I could do was smile and say, "Yeah, well, you know . . ."

CHAPTER 5

Serial Heartbreaker

I'll admit it. I was a serial heartbreaker. I was only up for a sexual thrill. After Paul, I jumped right into two more long-term relationships in a row—with Clayton and Roland. And I can't believe I was engaged to them both. They were hollow engagements, though. I said yes, took the ring, played the fiancée role, but I never really planned to live my life with either man. Poor fellows. They never saw it coming.

But before those two ill-fated back-to-back engagements, I had a sexual experience that would send me further in a direction that I seemed destined for anyway. I'd had my first taste of voyeurism when I fucked Alberto in front of Cole in Tokyo. But that was just the tip of the iceberg when it came to my desire to be watched, to let strangers in on my most intimate moments, and to be the fantasy girl that only some can touch. I let that freak flag fully fly when I met a fireman from Boise, Idaho, when I was eighteen. I'd moved to Boise the year prior to move back in with my father, who was teaching at the University of Idaho at the time.

The fireman (whose name I don't remember) and I were just having a casual fling and one night I visited him at the firehouse. I wore a pair of white lacy panties because I wasn't planning on being a bad girl that night. To this day, I always wear white or pink panties when I feel like being good and red or black panties when I'm feeling ultra slutty and bad. When I got there, he was in an especially frisky mood.

He took me aside and asked, "Hey Linda, can the guys watch us have sex and jerk off to us?"

"Ewww. Nooooo!" I replied, completely disgusted.

"Come on, girls never come over here," he said.

"They can watch, but they can't jerk off," I said.

The idea of some of the guys watching us fuck turned me on . . . a lot. It's funny the lines that I draw: watching is OK, but watching and jerking off is not OK. When it was just one guy (Cole in Tokyo), it was OK, but the idea of a group of guys jerking off to me fucking, well, that just seemed wrong. Yeah, it seems arbitrary now, but it made sense to me in the moment. Regardless, it was a huge turn-on to have them watching me, staring at me, and wanting me but not being able to have me.

My fireman fuck buddy peeled my clothes off in front five or so other guys and positioned me with my hands on the wall in standing doggy position. As he fucked me from behind, I looked over my shoulder to make fuck-me eyes at the guys, who were really into it. They were cheering us on with "oh yeahs." That turned me on even more. I loved performing for people. I fucking loved being the object of their erections! That was truly the start of my desire to fuck for the world to see.

When I left the firehouse that night, I left my man those white panties, and a few days later he showed up to my place with a box of doughnuts. Not exactly a fair exchange, but it was sweet. I soon dumped him because I just got bored, and then I met Clayton.

Clayton was twelve years older than me. I was eighteen; he was thirty. He was a rock-and-roll car nut. He had a car- and bike-building business, was a tough guy, and was financially independent. The independence was what attracted me to him. He was a father figure, in a way. I was looking, once again, for a man to make me feel secure and loved. I wasn't feeling strong enough to take care of myself, so I looked to men to do it for me.

I was still young, rebellious, and sex-crazed with raging hormones. My hormones were so in control that I ended up cheating on dear Clayton because he wasn't giving me enough sex. My sexual appetite was insatiable. Clayton treated me well and I broke his heart. I do feel bad about that. I obviously hurt him a lot, because he made me pay him $1,500 to buy back some of my old modeling photos he had of me.

The first guy to match my sexual appetite was my next boyfriend, Roland. Roland was a wild, sexy, perverted real estate guy who lived in a huge house in Victorville, California, where I moved after my break-up with Clayton to live with my father once again, who had, once again moved due to a new job. (This time it was a trucking gig.) Roland made the fatal mistake of moving me to Los Angeles with him when I was just twenty-one years old. Los Angeles was a place where I could (and would) get into a lot of trouble. It had the same fast life I loved in Tokyo—the shopping, the partying, the hot rocker boys, and the proximity to the entertainment business.

Roland opened me up to a whole new sexual world. We started making home sex tapes and took pornographic photos. I loved having sex for the camera, but at the time I never thought I'd do it professionally. It was just our dirty little secret. It turned me on to see a photo of his cock in my pussy or photos of me with a dildo. I'd always had this really nasty sexual side to me, but Roland was the first guy to truly unleash that beast.

He also introduced me to porn. I'd never watched porn before I met Roland. The first video I ever watched was titled *Café Flesh*, a 1982 postapocalyptic sci-fi film that was a cult favorite. It featured a beautiful actress named Pia Snow and was cowritten by Jerry Stahl, who went on to write the book and movie *Permanent Midnight* and that '80s show *ALF*. And the first porn magazine I ever saw was at Roland's house. I'm talking the real, hardcore porno magazines, not the *Playboy* or *Penthouse* I was used to seeing. I don't remember the name of the magazine, but I'll never forgot how turned on I was by a photo spread with Shayla LaVeaux. She was blond and gorgeous.

It was all about kinky first-times with Roland. He was the first guy I had anal sex with as well. It hurt, of course, but I liked it. He introduced me to anal beads and other kinky stuff, like the time he put my pearl necklace in my butt and then made me wear it around my neck when we went to dinner that night with his parents. I was so turned on watching Roland stare at my dirty necklace during that dinner. Roland's also the guy who shaved my pussy bald. I had a bush before I met him!

But all kinky things must come to an end. Roland started getting into heavy drugs like crystal meth and cocaine, and I wasn't down with that. I never have been and never will be into hard drugs. The drugs made him abusive, and one day he hit me. I moved out immediately, broke off our engagement, and left. No guy's ever going to fucking hit me, and no man ever did again.

It was time to move on anyway. New cock. New life. After Roland, I just took guys home randomly when I needed to get fucked. I'd grab a guy and say, "You're coming home with me. I'm fucking you." No man said no.

Chapter 6

From Bedpans to Bedrooms

After a few years of meandering through life, I decided it was time to stop fucking around and get serious. At age eighteen, I spent a week studying for my GED and passed it on the first try at Boise State University, and began my undergraduate studies in nursing there. I transferred to the American Institute of Health Technology, also in Boise, where I earned an emergency medical technical (EMT) certificate and trained to be a nurse.

Dad was finally proud of me, and I was finally settling down and growing up. No more self-indulgent wild ways. It was all about being of service to others for a change. I worked most days as a telemarketer for a security-alarm-system company. It was my first time dealing with rejection: I got hung up on a lot! And I went to school at night. I moved back to California after school because I found a job at a nursing home in Simi Valley. At first I really loved working with old people and was good at it. So good that I remember my dad telling me one day, "I don't fear getting old because I know you're going to take such good care of me." That made me feel good. It was nice to have Dad back in my life again.

The nursing work came easily to me at first. I loved to knit, so in the wintertime I would knit lap blankets for my patients, and in the morning instead of just giving them their meds and pushing my medicine cart to the next room, I would sit down and talk with them and brush their hair and put on their makeup, or even do some exercise with them. I was all about engaging my patients. It felt good to be good.

It also felt good to be around hot doctors, whom I flirted with shamelessly. The other nurses would often tease me about what a big flirt I was and say things like, "Oh, Linda. You belong in front of the camera." Or, "Oh, Linda, you should model." I didn't have the heart to tell them that I tried modeling. I was embarrassed to let them know I blew it. Besides, I was enjoying my new life. For the first time, I didn't have to watch my weight and I wasn't messed up on drugs and alcohol. At age twenty-two, I was finally feeling pretty happy and normal.

But as time went on, the work became a little more difficult and a lot more depressing. There were still a lot of great patients whom

From my nursing days

I enjoyed helping, but the day-in, day-out nature of the job started to take a toll on me. My breaking point came one day with one of my regular patients—a woman named Catherine, who was in her mid-seventies and had a bad case of Alzheimer's. She was demanding every single kind of drug under the sun. I helped her as much as I could, but she just kept hitting her call light and demanding more. At one point, she put on her light and asked me to put her on the bedpan, which I did. Normally, another nurse would have come in a few minutes later to remove it. But the nurse ignored the light. An hour or so later, I saw her call light was going off again. I was about to leave for lunch, but I felt really bad for her and I thought to myself, "I'll stop by her room one last time and see what she needs before I go."

I walked into her room and before I could even ask her what she needed, she took her bedpan from underneath her and threw it at me. She might have been an old lady, but she had a good arm—it was a direct hit. I was standing there, soaked in her urine, and she told me, "That's what you get for not coming back on time."

I thought to myself, "Oh my God. This just did not happen to me." In that moment, I was deeply humbled. Here is a woman who can't go to the bathroom on her own and the only way to communicate with me is to throw a fucking bedpan at my head. It felt awful. I wiped the urine off my face and decided in that moment that there had to be something better for me out there. I took the rest of the day off and I quit my job the very next day. It was the spring of 1999 and time for a fresh start.

I had been living in an apartment in Canoga Park, California, a city in the Valley—the porn capital of the world. It was a small place, but for my friends and me it was our dream pad—a real party apartment. My girlfriends would drop by all the time to hang out there. When I arrived home soaked in urine that day and ready for a shower, two friends were waiting for me: Elena, a hairdresser, and Honey, a photographer. I told them what had just happened, and we began brainstorming about what else I could do with my life. Naturally, the talk turned to modeling. Honey said, "I think you should pose for *Playboy*. I think that it would be an amazing opportunity for you."

I had never done nude modeling before, but the idea appealed to me. I was an exhibitionist and, of course, I grew up loving those girls in *Playboy*. Elena wasn't so sure. "I think you're too good to do *Playboy*," she said. "I think it's degrading to women. I don't think you should do it." I didn't think it was degrading to women. I figured if nude modeling was good enough for my idols, then it was good enough for me.

At the time, I was a size 6 and 135 pounds. That was way too large to go back to runway, print, or commercial modeling. You need to be about 110 at my height for that kind of modeling. But you *can* be a size 6 or even larger to pose in *Playboy* or other nude magazines, and that is what I love about that part of the industry. You don't have to be stick thin to show the world you're beautiful. This was a door that was open to someone like me, so I ran through that door with my arms and legs wide open.

Nude modeling and porn are the only areas of the entertainment industry that seemed to truly embrace women of all sizes, shapes, colors, and backgrounds. Hollywood makes you conform to being that size 0, but porn and slutty magazines don't. It's an equal-opportunity industry. In mainstream Hollywood, a woman like me—half Thai, size 6, big double-D natural breasts—wouldn't get work. The real Hollywood discriminates. But the *other* Hollywood—the sexier side of Tinseltown—welcomes all. Marilyn Monroe and Bettie Page weren't stick figures and they got tons of work, so I learned to enjoy my voluptuous body. I liked being curvy, just like my idols.

I wanted to be part of this other side of Hollywood. I didn't care that Elena thought *Playboy* wasn't good enough for me. I made my decision. I filled out the application and made an appointment down at Playboy Studio West in Santa Monica, California. I was interviewed by a woman named Stephanie, who was impressed by my modeling résumé and my look. She told me, "Wow, you are so beautiful. We're going to do a test shoot with you next week and we'll let you know right away."

For the test shoot, which was in May 1999, I wore a casual summer dress and sandals. I'd put on my best thong underwear and made sure not to wear a bra so I could really show off my boobs. As we were about to shoot, I got worried that I wasn't dressed well enough. Stephanie told me, "Oh, no, don't worry. We're going to put you in a pretty little outfit and we're going to do your hair and makeup."

"Perfect." I felt at ease and excited at the same time.

As I walked down the hallways of Playboy West Studios to the dressing room, I saw pictures all over the walls of various beautiful girls, one after the other, including Marilyn Monroe. That really clinched it for me.

The makeup artist was a really sweet girl named Kimberly. She started playing with my hair. She picked up a handful and said, "Wow, you have just about the thickest hair I've ever seen on any girl."

I wondered whether that was a good thing or a bad thing.

She sat me down in the chair and she put my hair in hot rollers and started painting my face. They brought me a cup of tea, a Coke, and some iced coffee and got me all jacked up. Then they took me to the wardrobe room and picked out a sexy, matching black bra-and-panty set for me.

My strongest memory of the studio is how cold it was. It was a hot summer day outside, but it was ice cold in there. In the middle of the studio was a giant bed with big fluffy pillows surrounded by big beautiful lights. I'd been a little nervous about being in front of the camera again—it had been six years since I'd done any modeling. But I have to say that modeling is like riding a bike. I just automatically fell back into it. They asked me to lie on the bed and I did, arching my back, looking right into the camera. It felt so natural, just like my first test shoot but more glamorous.

The photographer's only direction to me was this: "OK, this is for your expression: I want lots of 'Ooohs' and lots of 'Ahhhs.' 'Oooh. Ahhh.' Get it?"

I got it. And for the next twenty minutes I went "oooh" and "ahhh" and it was a lot of fun. It was an amazing feeling being in front of the camera again, and I really enjoyed it. It felt like being a princess for a day. After that, I went to my little Mazda 323 hatchback and called my friend Honey. "Well, I did it. I wonder what they're going to say."

She was confident. "Oh, they're going to pick you for sure."

Sure enough, I got a call the very next day. It was Stephanie: "We'd like to have a meeting with you to talk about being in *Playboy*." They wanted me! I was thrilled. I couldn't believe it. We set up a meeting for the following Monday. I was on my way.

As if fate knew what I was about to do, that same week I saw an ad for figure models at Jim South's World Modeling Agency on Van Nuys Boulevard in Van Nuys, California, and I walked right in. I figured if *Playboy* wanted me, other magazines would too. So I marched into World Modeling's offices in these super-short white denim shorts, a baby blue tank top, and heels, looking like Miss Slutterina, and told them I wanted to model.

"Oh my God. Who are *you*?" said a woman in her late twenties named Chazz. She was Jim South's receptionist, and I'd later find out that she was a performer in the porn industry too. I'd also later find out that World Modeling didn't just rep girls for nude magazines, but for adult films as well.

"I'm Linda. I'm here for the figure modeling."

Chazz must have liked what she saw because she immediately took me into one of the back rooms and Polaroided me. That's what they did back then. They would take quick Polaroid photos to get a feel for how you photograph. She took a few shots from the front, a few from the back, a few from the side, and then said, "I can definitely get you in *Penthouse*."

"*Penthouse?* Oh my God," I thought to myself.

"When can I get in *Penthouse*?" I asked Chazz.

"I'm going to call photographer Suze Randall. She shoots for the magazine. She'll shoot you and then submit the photos to *Penthouse* and we'll see*."

"Great!" I couldn't believe it. *Playboy* and *Penthouse*?!

A few days later, I went to Suze Randall's studio on Kotner in Santa Monica, California. Suze is this wonderful dykey woman with cropped blond hair like Victoria Beckham, schoolmarmish glasses, and a charming thick British accent. I showed up in a matching peach bra and thong set and asked, "Do you want me to get naked?" I was ready to bare all.

"No, darling," Suze said. "Keep your clothes on this time." She took ten photos of me in my bra and panties and said, "Oh yeah. We're getting you in *Penthouse*. I'm shooting you next week."

She followed through. We shot that Friday for *Penthouse*. It was just a few days before my scheduled Monday meeting with *Playboy*. I couldn't believe it was happening so fast. All I could think was, "I'm going to be in *Playboy* and *Penthouse*, make tons of money, and be famous!" This was my second chance at modeling and my ticket back. I was filled with a newfound optimism about my career and my life.

The shoot for *Penthouse* was unlike any shoot I had done up to that point. It was at Suze's ranch in Calabasas, California, and it was the biggest, most glamorous shoot I'd ever done. I was so thrilled to have Emma Nixon, one of the most highly regarded makeup and hairstylists in the industry, do my hair and makeup. She worked with everyone. I was floored that the same woman who helped make

Pamela Anderson look so beautiful was working on me, too. I felt like I was finally at the level I always wanted to be.

The problem was that I had no idea what I was doing. Sure, I had modeled before, but never completely naked! For instance, I had no idea I was supposed to spread my pussy. I'm starting to pose for photos and I'm just lying there with my legs wide open, thinking this was how you do it. The next thing I know, Suze takes a Q-tip covered in baby oil and she starts petting my pussy with it. She stroked the lips, she stroked the inside edge, she stroked around the outside of my pussy with this moist little Q-tip.

"Pinky, pinky, pinky," Suze was saying in that British accent of hers.

"Pinky?" What the hell is she saying?

"Yes, darling, you need to show your pussy. We need to see more pink. Pinky, pinky, pinky!"

I had no idea you had to, as Suze said, get the pussy all "shiny and glistening and inviting." That's where the baby oil came in.

With my pussy moistened, open, and ready to be properly photographed, I really got into the shoot. But every time Suze would remind me to "show more pink," I would laugh my ass off. As she shot me, she would say things to coax the sex kitten out of me, such as "Come on, you little slut. Open your legs, you little slut. Let's see the pink!" Thinking about it now, it sounds so vulgar but at the time she sounded very charming and posh in that British accent, and I couldn't help but giggle every time she said "pinky, pinky, pinky."

Suze and I got along great and I was excited to share my other news with her. I told her that I was meeting with Stephanie at *Playboy* on Monday to discuss shooting for them. That was the biggest mistake, because after hearing this news Suze rushed the layout to *Penthouse* to make sure that her spread would get published.

That Monday, I walked into *Playboy* to see Stephanie and she showed me the contract for me to pose for the magazine. I didn't know anything about contracts, but as I was reading it over it sounded too good to be true: $25,000 for a week's worth of work! I mentioned to Stephanie that $25,000 was practically a year's pay at the nursing home and that I was only paid $5,000 for *Penthouse*.

Suze Randall

"Um, *Penthouse*?" said Stephanie as she took the contract away. "You can't be in *Playboy* if you are in *Penthouse*. That's how it goes. Sorry."

I quickly got on the phone with Suze and tried to stop the *Penthouse* spread, but it was too late. The *Penthouse* spread was a done deal and I was fucked. I walked out of *Playboy*'s offices in tears and cried myself to sleep that night. It wasn't until years later when I became a famous porn star that I would have my shot at *Playboy* again. And that time, I ended up on the cover of *Penthouse* and *Playboy* within a month of each other, becoming the only girl in history who has ever done that. So, all's well that ends well. But that day in *Playboy*'s Santa Monica studio, I felt like someone just punched me in the stomach.

I decided to suck it up. It wasn't a total loss. I mean, *Penthouse* was a huge magazine too. And Suze Randall told me there was more where that came from. She said, "I'll put you in every nude magazine out there." So, that's what I did. I became a nude model, and I was Suze's muse.

CHAPTER 7

My Arousal

Within my first year of nude modeling for magazines like *Penthouse, Hustler, High Society, Club,* and *Cheri,* I got a phone call from a man named Andrew Blake. He's a very artistic filmmaker who makes beautiful fetish and softcore erotica movies. To this day, he's considered the most artistic director of adult films. His first film, *Night Trips* in 1989, was given a silver medal at the WorldFest-Houston International Film Festival, making it the *only* porn movie to win a medal at a major international film festival. If you wanted to make a beautiful film, Andrew Blake was the man to work with.

Needless to say, when Andrew called, I freaked out. He told me, "I have seen your work in all the magazines and I'm interested in filming you in one of my movies."

I was so flattered that he knew my work that I didn't hesitate. "OK," I immediately replied.

"Are you sure?" he asked. He must have been shocked at how easy it was for me to say yes.

I'd never really thought about doing movies before, but the idea instantly appealed to me. Right then and there, I was ready to make the leap. I told him, "Yeah, I'm ready to do something different. I'm ready to live out some of my fantasies. I'm in."

And that was the truth about why I wanted to do porn. It really was all about the sex for me, and about acting out my sexual fantasies. Unlike so many girls in the industry, I got into porn for the right reasons.

Yes, there are right reasons and wrong reasons to get into porn.

The Right Reasons to Get into Porn:

You love sex and are turned on by doing it in front of a camera.

You're a free spirit.

You don't give a fuck what other people think about you.

You love the money.

You feel empowered, not degraded.

The Wrong Reasons to Get into Porn:

Your boyfriend made you do it.

Daddy didn't love you enough.

You have to support a drug habit.

You *need* the money.

You want to get into Hollywood. (Ladies, porn is *not*, I repeat *not*, the gateway to Hollywood!)

When Andrew told me that my part in the film *Aroused* would be glamorous girl-girl scenes, it sounded like the perfect opportunity to see if film work was for me. I told him right away that I was OK with having my pussy licked by a girl, but I didn't want to lick pussy. I didn't really know how to negotiate, but I knew enough to tell him what I would and wouldn't do in a film. I never let anyone talk me into anything I wasn't comfortable with. This film was like dipping my toe into a pool to test the water.

I went down to the *Aroused* set, which was at a beautiful mansion up on Cielo Drive off of Benedict Canyon in Beverly Hills. I was excited because Cielo Drive was also where the Tate Murder House was, which was where Charles Manson and his followers killed actress Sharon Tate and her friends. I was still obsessed with serial killers like I was when I was a young girl. I had read all about the Manson murders in *Helter Skelter* and now I was actually going to be able to see the house where the madness occurred. It didn't look as creepy as I thought it would on the outside; just your typical Beverly Hills ranch house.

When I got to the shoot, the other girls were already on the set and everyone welcomed me with open arms. I wasn't sure what I was getting myself into, but I wasn't afraid of it. I felt a strange kind of nervous excitement that just washed over me. I couldn't quite believe that I was about to do my first adult movie even though my scenes were pretty mild. They involved a lot of slow, soft, sensual petting, kissing, touching, and posing in erotic ways. No lines of dialogue, thank God, because I wasn't ready for that!

It felt like a real Hollywood movie set. The house was stunning. There were makeup artists, hairdressers, stylists, crew, and assistants everywhere. I remember being impressed by a plate of cut-up fruit and bottles of sparkling water. It was all very glamorous. And the scenes were beautiful. There was a lot of touching, teasing, and fondling, and many leg shots, boob shots, and vagina shots. It was beautiful, artistic, and erotic. If Fellini made porn, this would be what he'd have made. It was shot in both black and white and color, had a very surreal soundtrack and feel to it, and featured a lot of classic fetish elements, such as thigh-high latex boots, old-fashioned stockings, impossible-to-walk-in fetish heels, and dream sequences.

Andrew Blake was a very go-with-the-flow director. I remember him directing me by saying, "OK, we are now panning up the legs," and he let me move my legs however I wanted. I glided my right foot over my left leg and he seemed pleased by that. Then he handed me a cigarette from off-camera and just said, "OK, smoke" and I looked into the camera and smoked in a sensuous way. And then he took the cigarette away and gave me a razor and put shaving cream on my legs and said, "OK, shave your legs." So I shaved my legs in the sexiest way I could. (That scene got cut, by the way.) Andrew had the cutest name for the pussy. He called it a fui-fui. So, he'd say, "OK, now we're panning down to the fui-fui." And I'd run my hand over my fui-fui. I wanted to laugh. But I stayed professional.

My first scene with another girl was with a performer named Dahlia Grey, who was Andrew's muse and the main star of the movie. She was exotic-looking like me, and Andrew thought we'd look great together. We did. We had several scenes together and even kissed. I had never been with a girl before, but kissing isn't exactly "being with a girl." We kissed and fondled each other, and at once point I even kissed her pussy, but I never went down on her. There was no actual sex or penetration, so my scenes were considered softcore. One of my big scenes was titled "Sliced Fruit" and they laid me down on the floor with a flower in my hair and juicy exotic fruit on my pussy. A Russian performer whose real name was Lucy (I forget her stage name) ate me out while Dahlia felt me up. It was my first time having a girl go down on me. I had never been with a girl before, but as long as she was doing the licking, I was fine with it. I was excited to do it, actually. But the unknown was a bit scary for me. I didn't know if after the scene I'd want to go home and fuck her or just shake hands and say good-bye. We ended up just shaking hands and saying good-bye. This doesn't really count as my first girlie scene, since it wasn't hardcore. That comes later.

For one of our scenes, we were both wearing super high heels—twelve-inch heels, the kind I'd seen Bettie Page wear in her fetish films. On the first take, we were walking down the side of the house and I tripped and fell. Lucy and I had a good laugh about that. But we got it right for the next take. And then we swam in a pool together. It was a beautiful, in-ground pool, with glass panels that you could see through. The scene felt very sterile and cold, and I didn't cum. Part of the problem was the set: it was a modern, stone house with a waterfall and koi pond. And part of it was because there wasn't any sexual tension. I wasn't into girls. Cock got me off, not pussy. So to help motivate me, I imagined that my dream guy—at this time it was Johnny Depp—was looking at me through the lens, and that I was trying to impress him. That's how I got myself through my scenes.

It was a four-day shoot (twelve hours a day), and every night I came home exhausted, but elated. I would lie in bed and think to myself, "OK, I made $3,500 today. Tomorrow, I'm going to make another $3,500, and then for the box cover the third day I'm going to make $5,000, and that's going to be a total of $12,000! And I'm going to be able to pay my rent and finally buy those new Gucci shoes I've been wanting. And then maybe I'll get rid of that little Mazda hatchback and buy a new car." My thoughts were racing. I wanted to live life on my own terms, and this felt like the way to get me there.

I wasn't at all bothered at the thought of getting naked for the camera. I wasn't hurting myself or doing anything degrading. I felt like I was doing something really beautiful. There was no real sex, just a little bit of pussy licking. This was certainly not Hollywood, but it was the *other* Hollywood, and it suited me just fine. That said, I kept my on-screen activities as my dirty little secret. If my best friend Elena thought I was too good for *Playboy*, what would she think if I told her I was doing a porno movie? I wasn't going to find out. So I didn't tell anyone.

I went home from the *Aroused* set so horny because we did everything but sex in the movie and it made me crave a man. So I went home to my apartment in Canoga Park and knocked on my neighbor's door and said, "Hi. I'm Tera. Want to fuck?" I don't even remember his name, but he got me through that four-day shoot.

A week or so after we wrapped up the movie, I got a call from a woman named Patty Rhodes, who used to work for Andrew Blake. She had gone out on her own as a producer and heard about the work I had been doing.

"I hear you're doing movies now," she said.

"Well, sort of."

"I know your work as a model, and I'd love to include you in one of my movies. I would like to make you an offer to do a boy-girl movie with me for Adam and Eve Productions called *Fire and Ice*. Is that OK or do you just do girl-girl?"

I had no idea what she was talking about. Porn terms weren't exactly part of my lingo yet. Girl-girl? Boy-girl?

"What do you mean?" I asked.

"Well, you would have sex with a guy instead of a girl," she explained.

"Oh, that's awesome. I would love to be with a guy! Oh, it's so weird for me to be with a girl. I like guys better than girls."

Most girls starting out in the industry do girl-girl films for a few months before diving into boy-girl films, but not me. I was ready to do a real fuck film right away, so I said yes without hesitation. Knowing what I know now about the industry, this must have been music to her ears.

I honestly never thought, and still don't think, that there was anything wrong with having sex for money on camera. It's not too far off from prostitution and that is, as they say, the world's oldest and most honest profession. Any living is an honest one if you're doing it because you want to do it.

My saying is this: "We're all ho's on this bus."

I don't judge anyone. It's funny because in this business the *Playboy* Playmates judge the *Penthouse* Pets. The *Penthouse* Pets judge the porn stars. The porn stars judge the hookers. But we're all ho's on this bus. What is the difference if you're a high-class, high-paid call girl sleeping with a rich guy for $10,000 or you're doing a porn movie scene for $10,000? It's the same. I truly don't think porn or prostitution should be frowned upon.

So I went to visit Patty the next day at her house and we talked about the scene. She said my costar would be with a guy named Brick Majors, and she showed me his picture. I thought he was kind of cute. Then she talked money with me.

"We're willing to pay you top dollar for this," she said. "Twenty-five hundred for just a couple of hours of work."

"Great. Sign me up!" I said.

I showed up on the set the next night at seven p.m. and was taken aback when I first laid eyes on my costar. Brick came out of the trailer and he looked like a Ken doll come to life. He was really tan and muscular with bleached, spiky hair. My first thought was, "Oh my God. This guy wears more makeup than me and he's tanner than I am. He's even in better shape than me. What the hell am I going to do?"

He walked over to me and shook my hand. "Hi, Tera. I'm Brick. I'm happy that we're going to be working together." He was so nice and professional, but I began to feel some butterflies in my stomach. This was a big leap. Posing nude is one thing. Doing girl-on-girl porn is another. But this was the real deal—I was about to make a hardcore adult film with a man. I remember thinking to myself, "OK. Here's where the switch comes in. I just have to turn that switch on, and I just have to have sex. This is easy. I can do this."

But really, I had no idea what I was doing or how to prepare for a scene. I brushed my teeth before my first scene with Brick, and the director yelled at me. "No. No. You're supposed to use mouthwash. If you use a toothbrush, you might get microscopic cuts in your mouth, and that's not safe."

I had no idea what the positions were either. I was really winging it. I got my script and it said "reverse cowgirl," and I was like a deer caught in headlights. "Huh? Reverse what?" I asked.

"It's like cowgirl, but backwards," said the director, Nicholas Steele, who was a blond, Californian surfer-looking guy.

"Cowgirl backwards? So my back faces him?! Oh my God! How do I prop myself up?"

The cameraman had to walk me through every position. I told him, "Listen, this is my first movie. I don't know what any of these positions are."

He told me, "Don't worry. I'll show you before we get to each scene."

Once I got famous, I refused to do reverse cowgirl again. I just don't have the leg strength for that. It's a hard position for a girl. It's quite the workout, and I hated to work out. I became known as a "pillow queen." A pillow queen is a porn girl who just gets fucked and looks beautiful and doesn't do as much of the hardcore work. I was fine with that.

Porn Sex Positions:

- **COWGIRL:** The woman sits on top of the guy, facing him.

- **REVERSE COWGIRL:** The woman sits on top of the guy with her back to him. This is a director's dream, but an actress's worst nightmare.

- **PILE DRIVER:** The woman lies on her back with her legs over her head, and the guy is on top and over her.

- **MISSIONARY:** Same as your regular missionary, but to get a good angle on a porn shoot, the girl usually has to put her leg up on his shoulder and the other leg is open wide to the camera.

- **DOGGY-STYLE:** Doggy-style in porn can be any number of ways where the guy takes you from behind. You can be on all fours. You can be standing. You can be kneeling. You can even be leaning up on a wall.

- **SPOON:** He lies behind you and you're lying side-by-side. It's like spooning when you cuddle, but with a penis inside you.

- **SCISSORS:** This is usually associated with lesbian sex where two girls are touching pussy-to-pussy with their legs in an open scissor position. For a guy and girl, the girl lies on her side with her legs open and the guy is either kneeling or standing and inserts himself inside her.

Even though he looked like a Ken doll and that wasn't exactly my type, I found it easy to get aroused by Brick. It felt oddly natural to me. I wasn't very sexually active at this time in my life, so I was pretty excited to just be having sex. Even while I was doing magazines, I decided that I was going to be single so that I didn't have the distraction of a boyfriend. Instead, I wanted to devote my time to building my career. As I did more movies, I would get so excited before going to work. "Woo-hoo! I'm getting laid today! Plus I'm getting $1,000! Yeah!" Money really is a powerful aphrodisiac.

When the time came for our scene, I didn't need any lube because I was naturally wet from being so excited to fuck on camera.

I moved onto my hands and knees on this little stage area to get into the first position: doggy-style. But when I reached around the back to get more traction by grabbing onto his leg, I immediately pulled my hand away. His leg felt like wax and it kind of freaked me out. I hadn't noticed that he was completely hairless, and that waxed leg felt like a mannequin's. I had never been with a guy who had shaved his legs before. It was the weirdest feeling that I had ever felt in my life. I thought, "What *is* this? This guy is smooth like a baby! He's smoother than me!"

Between getting used to a porn guy's shaved legs (I later found out that was pretty common for porn guys) and learning how to do all of these sex positions, I was pretty out of my element. Luckily, there wasn't much acting. The only direction I got was the director saying, "We need to hear more from you. Say more!" I didn't know what to say, so I remembered the direction I got on my *Playboy* shoot, so I started going "Oooh" and "Ahhh." That seemed to do the trick. The director was happy.

Getting penetrated on film for the first time was a bit shocking to me. I was super excited by it and really into the scene, but at the same time I felt vulnerable at having all of these people watching me. Some people can't even be seen in public in a bathing suit, but here I am getting fucked by a Ken doll on camera. I knew that I was not like the average girl. Things like this turned me on. I wasn't ashamed. I wanted more. At the same time, I was blown away by my own decision to do this. I kept thinking to myself, "This is crazy. This is crazy. This is crazy."

We finished, shook hands, and my day's work was completed. It was all very cordial. Leaving the set that night, I was pretty excited. Working with Brick had been a real pleasure. Everyone involved in the production was very nice to me. Patty Rhodes and I became friends. I ended up working for her a lot.

"So, what do you think?" Patty asked me post-shoot.

"It was fun. But you know, Brick isn't really my type. I like it a bit rougher," I said.

"Don't worry, girl. I've got plenty of guys that will be your type," Patty said.

At about two a.m., I headed home and went to bed. It had all been pretty exhausting, but it was worth it. The money was great and I had fun. I tossed and turned all night thinking, (a) I can't believe I just did that and (b) I can't wait to do it all over again.

CHAPTER 8

Get It Up. Get It In.
Get It Off. Get It Out.

Peaple say porn is degrading to women. I'm no fool. Of course, porn *can* be degrading to women. Some pornos have scenes in which a man steps on a woman's head, which may sound freaky to you but is pretty common in the industry. It's not one I've ever done because, to me, it *is* degrading. In other movies the men spit on women, but I won't let anyone spit on me. Double and triple anal isn't for me either. Putting two or three cocks in a woman's ass is solely about degrading her. One is enough for me. Some girls don't like getting a facial (that's when a guy cums all over your face). But that's a big turn-on for me. It's so dirty that it's hot, and I didn't care if it ruined my makeup. There was only one rule: don't shoot me in the eye. But it's happened by accident and I didn't have any hard feelings. I just said, "Get me a baby wipe, please," and continued on. I have my rules, I play by them, I make others follow them, and the consequence is that I don't get hurt. It's really been as simple as "A, B, C, don't fuck with me."

I won't put myself in any scene that I don't fully enjoy doing, and I always make sure my movies are beautiful. I got into porn because I was a twenty-two-year-old free spirit who loved to get her freak on, live out wild sexual fantasies, and feel beautiful and desired. And frankly, I just love to get fucked. And it got me off. I didn't have to fake orgasms because I was really into the sex and it was an extra turn-on to have people watching me have sex. That made me cum hard. It is empowering for me, not degrading. I can't say what's right and wrong for other girls. Maybe some girls actually enjoy getting spit on, and if that's the case, then I don't judge them. But I know what makes me feel good and what makes me feel bad and throughout my entire ten years of doing porn, I never said yes to anything that I didn't fully and wholeheartedly want to do. Unfortunately, not all girls in porn can say the same thing and those are the films that give porn a bad name.

My Sexual Likes:

- Rough sex
- Hair-pulling
- Mild choking
- Getting tied up
- Playing the submissive
- Strong, tough, tattooed men

My Sexual Dislikes:

- Head-stepping
- Spitting
- Slapping (well, sometimes)
- Double anything
- Girlie-guys

With my rules firmly in place and a true excitement for the industry, I hit the ground running hard. Between June and December of 1999, I was shooting two or three times a week, making $15,000 a month, and had amassed a collection of about forty movies, including *Sex Island, Up and Cummers, Foot Lovers Only, The Video Ad-*

ventures of Peeping Tom 22, Farmer's Daughters Do Beverly Hills, and others. I upgraded my car from a Mazda 323 hatchback to a much nicer Honda Accord and moved out of my little apartment in Canoga Park to a fancier loft in Woodland Hills, California. I also discovered Rodeo Drive in Beverly Hills and could finally afford Gucci and Prada instead of Forever 21 and Steve Madden. I even upgraded my name. My given name, Linda Ann Hopkins, wasn't going to cut it in this industry, so after trying out a few stage names, I settled on Tera Patrick.

SAY MY NAME:

Here's the history of my various names over the years:

LINDA ANN HOPKINS: This is my birth name. My parents actually considered naming me Florida. Yes, Florida, as in the Sunshine State. It fit with Dad's hippie style, but Mom

On the set of Caribbean Undercover *in 1999*

thought it might be too weird and liked the name Linda because it means "beautiful" in Spanish. The nurse asked, "So, is it Florida or Linda?" and Mom just settled on Linda. It was a popular name at the time.

BROOKE MACHADO: I used this name for the foot fetish film, *Foot Lovers Only.* I just liked the name Brooke for a first name, so I used that. The photographer thought I looked Brazilian and said it would be cool if people thought I was from Brazil so he gave me the last name Machado.

BROOKE THOMAS: I was shooting my very first photo layout with Suze Randall for *Club* magazine and the photographer's name was Chris Thomas. He asked me to come up with a name that I liked and I said Brooke and I liked his last name, so Brooke Thomas was born. I used this name for the movie *Real Sex Magazine 22* as well.

SADIE JORDAN: This name was given to me for the movie *Paradise Hotel* and I don't even remember how or why I got the name. Sometimes they just put random names on the DVD box. They do that all the time. I'm also credited as Sadie Jordan for *Gallery of Sin* in 1999.

LINDA ANN SHAPIRO: I never went by the name Linda Ann Shapiro. Wikipedia.org got that wrong!

TARA PATRICK: Misspelling! My name was misspelled as Tara instead of Tera for *Crossroads, Aroused,* and *Real Sex Magazine 23*, both in 1999, and maybe a few others.

TERA PATRICK: I loved the name Tera because "terra" means Earth. And when I found out Carmen Electra's real name is Tara (with an "a" not an "e") Patrick, that made it even better. Who wouldn't want to be named after a sex symbol like her? I began doing business as Tera Patrick in 1999, but I didn't legally change my name to Tera Patrick until April 3, 2009.

In 1999 I was feeling like a hot, young chick on my own, and for the first time I felt responsible and in charge of my life. And I felt beautiful and confident. I thought, "It doesn't get any better than this! I get free sex with no strings attached. And I get paid good money to do something I love." I was enjoying life. I was free. And I was horny. My motto was: "Get it up. Get it in. Get it off. Get it out." That was my attitude on and off the set. I just didn't want a boyfriend at the time. I threw my idea of getting married out the window for a few years and focused on having fun and making money instead.

Three shoots stood out the most in 1999. They involved rough sex, a *Lost in Translation* moment, and Jenna Jameson and a big black dildo. Let me fill you in.

As Sadie Jordan in Paradise Hotel

One of my dirty little secrets is that I really do enjoy rough sex, but only to an extent. And it's hard to articulate what that line is until someone crosses it. Well, a porn actor who I'd rather not name in this story stepped over that line on the set of a film I refuse to name as well. He was a Puerto Rican performer who is known for being a little rough with girls and he treated me no different. I told him I liked it rough, and I didn't mind his hands on my throat or him pulling my hair. But he did it a little too hard. He touched me a little too rough. He grabbed my hair a little too tightly. He just did everything a little too much.

But the worst part was the look in his eyes. I can normally look a man in the eyes and feel a connection. I can normally turn a guy on with that connection while we're having sex. But when I looked into his eyes, he wasn't there. He was blank. He had this look like he actually hated women and was fucking me out of hate, not out of lust or passion. He was a monster to me. I used my "switch" and just turned it off, did my job, and got through it. My fans tell me that scene is a hard one to watch. I don't know because I haven't watched it, but I'll never forget how I felt when I left that set.

That experience didn't dissuade me from doing more movies, though. I just learned to be more specific about what kind of rough sex I liked the next time I shot. And I learned that I could choose whom I want to, and don't want to, work with. I was the one in charge, and I never let anyone forget that.

On a lighter note, the funniest scene in my entire career happened on the set of *Angel Dust* with a Spanish performer named Nacho Vidal, who had the biggest cock I'd ever seen. He was the sweetest guy ever, but his English wasn't so great. During our scene, he had me from behind doggy-style, and I looked over at him and said, "Fuck me like a whore."

He obviously didn't hear me correctly or maybe he got the words confused because he started saying in his sexy porn voice, "OK, horse. You like that, horse? How's that feel, horse?"

I started to crack up. The crew started to crack up. The director lost it. And poor Nacho got very embarrassed and confused and asked, "What? What are you laughing at?"

"Oh, honey," I said to him. "I said *whore*, not horse."

We all just lost it. The poor guy was really sensitive about his English and he thought we were making fun of him. But it was too funny to not laugh.

My third most memorable moment of 1999 was a photo shoot I did with Jenna Jameson with the French magazine *Hot Video* for a sexy spread titled "The Blonde Is Not Enough." Jenna showed up with her then-boyfriend *four* hours late, but I didn't care. That just left more time for me in the makeup chair with Lee Garland, who was one of my favorite makeup artists. He painted the faces of every major star in the porn industry since the late '80s and he was known for making any girl look flawless.

Jenna and I got along great. We both joked around a lot and liked to have fun. So, for two hours, we goofed off for the cameras and had a blast. We had to act out all of these different sex positions together, including going down on each other and getting it on with a very large black dildo. We loved the dildo so much that in between photo set-ups, we'd take turns just sitting on it. Neither one of us wanted to take it out! We were cracking up the entire time, and comparing notes on how sore our necks each were from having to look up at the camera while eating each other's pussy. Yes, neck pain is just one of the hazards of our job.

She must have liked working with me, because before leaving the set that day she gave me some advice: "You should do this series called *Virtual Sex*. I just did it. It's with this woman Samantha Lewis of Digital Playground. She'll pay you really well for it."

"OK, Jenna. Thanks!" I replied.

An outtake from the Hot Video sessions

It was the second time that month that Samantha Lewis's name came up. Ron Atkinson, a director and production manager in the adult industry, called me one day out of the blue on my cell (which, I kid you not, had the last four digits 6969) and said he had a friend named Samantha who was interested in doing a movie with me and that she pays top dollar.

I was always interested in working and was excited that both Jenna and Ron had vouched for this woman. A lot of money sounded good to me. The Van Nuys–based Digital Playground was a relatively new porn production company—it started just six years earlier in 1993. But if it was good enough for Jenna, it was good enough for me. I looked at it as just another movie, another fuck, and another day on a glamorous set. I was in.

So I met with Samantha and her partner at Digital Playground, Ali Joone, in December 1999 and shot *Virtual Sex with Tera Patrick* for them a week later. The Virtual Sex series is an interactive movie where you only see the girl performer and a guy's penis and the viewer takes the role of the male star and can dictate which sex acts he does with the female performer. Here's how it works: I welcome the viewer and invite him to control my actions by using buttons on his remote control. He can choose to have me tell him stories, perform foreplay, give him a blowjob, or have sex with him in a variety of positions. You can even choose the camera angles and

With Jenna in 2006

decide whether you want me to be naughty or nice. Porn has always been at the forefront of technology, and this was an exciting, groundbreaking new format to be a part of.

Samantha asked me how much I wanted to get paid for the movie and still not having a clue about the business, I said, "Oh, $5,000 would be good." Knowing what I know now, I probably could've said $50,000 since the video ended up being a top-selling DVD for the company. I even won an AVN Award for it for Best Interactive DVD. (The AVNs, put on by the industry trade magazine *Adult Video News*, are the Oscars of the porn industry and are held every January in Las Vegas.)

The movie turned out great, but it was not a fun shoot for me. I was not about making great movies at the time. I was about having great sex on camera, and this was not that. It was very technical and clinical and a tedious fifteen-hour workday. It was one of the hardest shoots I've ever done. I couldn't really get off in that film. There was too much stop/start, this angle/that angle, do this/do that. I couldn't just fuck, and that was frustrating for me.

The day after the shoot, Samantha asked me if I was under contract to anyone. I told her that I wasn't and Digital offered me a contract. I wasn't sure what to do so I talked my agent, Jim South, who was a good man with good advice. He was such a Southern gentleman. Jim was an older man with a lot of character in his face, slicked back hair, a big mustache, and talked with a soothing Southern drawl. "Well, you know, Tera," he said to me. "You've been working freelance and making good money. But you might do better if you were under contract."

He knew it was time for me to advance to the next level. I didn't call Digital Playground back right away. Instead, I decided to shop around and see what else was out there.

The first company I went to was Wicked Pictures in Canoga Park. They are known for their big, elaborate, cinematic feature films. They were the most "Hollywood" of all the porn companies and they had big-name contract girls like Jenna Jameson, Chasey Lain, and Alexa Rae in their stable. I met with the owner, Steve Orenstein, and he wanted to sign me right away. Jenna had just left the company and they were looking for the next big thing, and that was me. But Wicked wasn't right for me. I didn't want to be stuck only doing big, elaborate movies. I was not into feature films. I was into so-called gonzo films. I never wanted to be an actress. People want to see Angelina Jolie or Johnny Depp act and they want to see porn people fuck. I was into fucking. If I wanted to be an actress, then Wicked would've been the place to be. Everyone said I was too good for gonzo, but it's what I liked.

GONZO FILMS: These pornos are short on plot and long on close-ups of action. Gonzo films tend to run shorter than fea-

tures. They are typically shot with a single camera and a smaller crew, and the performer often acknowledges the camera. I love gonzo!

FEATURE FILMS: These have plots, dialogue, and often elaborate sets and storytelling. Features tend to run longer, have a larger crew, and be more complicated to shoot. I don't love features!

The next studio I checked out was Vivid Video. I liked Vivid because the two performers in the industry who I actually followed and admired were Kobe Tai and Janine Lindemulder and they were Vivid Girls. Kobe was a Taiwanese actress who I looked up to because she, like me, was Asian, and I thought if she could make it big as an Asian porn star, then maybe I could too. And Janine, well, Janine was so beautiful I could look at her for hours. I thought she was the most stunning porn actress in the industry. She has a really amazing face, and seemed like a true rebel with all her tattoos.

So, I met with Steve Hirsch, the owner of Vivid, who, by the way, is super cute. I had such a crush on him. He sat me down in front of his big desk. Twirling a phone cord nervously around his finger, he asked me, "So, what do you want to do? Do you want to be a contract girl? How many movies do you want to do? What are you willing to do?"

"Well, I don't know. You tell me what you want me to do," I said.

He said he'd want me to do twelve films a year, at $10,000 a film, which was a whopping $120,000, but he wanted me to do anal and DP (which means double penetration). I wasn't willing to do either one. I left Vivid's offices defeated. Vivid wasn't the place for me either. I was running out of studios.

"What am I going to do?" I wondered. I didn't fit in at Wicked.

I didn't fit in at Vivid. I didn't want to talk to other companies. Wicked and Vivid were the big two. And Digital Playground was the underdog, so I wasn't sure I wanted to be there, either.

I drank myself through New Year's Eve alone and made a resolution for the year 2000: Take it to the next level!

CHAPTER 9

The Secret's Out

After spending the better part of 1999 appearing spread-eagle for dozens of magazines and fucking on camera in dozens of porn films, I felt I had to let my family know what I was up to. But I wasn't quite ready to tell them the whole truth. It's one thing to *not* be ashamed of the dirty deeds I was doing; it's another thing to tell your father all about it. I didn't even want my dad to know I have sex, let alone that I was making a living by fucking. The thought mortified me. I wanted to be a virgin in my dad's eyes, and I wanted him to be proud of me. I'd always sought out his approval, and I knew I wouldn't be getting it for this. So, I decided to tell a little white lie.

It was around Christmas of 1999 and I was sitting on a cold park bench with my dad in Lakeport, California, where he was living at the time. (Dad moved around a lot.) I went home to visit him and my stepmom, Kara, for the holidays. He was clutching his dog's leash. Mick was a chocolate brown Irish terrier with wiry hair and this crazy Confucius beard. My dad was cool as usual. He was very relaxed. His legs were crossed and he was looking very proper. I was shaking partly because it was so cold outside and partly because of the bombshell I was about to unload.

"Dad, I've posed nude for magazines," I told him. "And I just want you to know it's my choice and I'm excited and it's going well."

His response shocked me: "Well, honey, you know there might be some people in that industry that might persuade you to do porn."

Porn! He brought up the porn! I thought, "Oh, this is going to be easier than I thought. Maybe I can tell him the whole truth."

Then he said, "I just want you to be careful. And don't let anyone do anything you don't want to do. Make all your decisions with a clear head."

"Oh my God. He knows! He knows everything," I immediately thought. My paranoid little mind was reeling. Dad's a hippie from the '60s. He knew I was a wild child and free spirited. I thought for sure he already knew. But he didn't say anything. I almost told him right then and there but something came over me and I chickened out. I didn't tell him I did porn until 2002 when my *Playboy* issue came out.

Meanwhile, my sister Debby found out on her own. Debby and her boyfriend walked into a video store one day and she saw a poster on the wall of me. My hair and makeup were really done up so it might have been hard to recognize me by face. But there was one telltale sign that proved it was me.

Debby told me she looked up at the poster and said to her boyfriend, "Oh my God. That's my fucking sister!"

"Your sister's name is Linda, not Tera," he said.

"No, that tattoo! She has a fuchsia rose tattoo on her right ankle. That is her! I would know that tattoo anywhere."

Debby called me that day and said, "I know exactly what you're up to and exactly what you're doing. You can't hide it from me."

I actually didn't want to hide it from her. My sister and I had been really close and I knew she was open-minded like me. I had planned on telling her first out of everyone in my family anyway. I just didn't get around to it. As I expected, Debby was totally cool with me being in porn. She always thought I should do something else in entertainment or modeling anyway. She told me, "As your sister I support you and I don't judge you. And if you can be happy with yourself and look in the mirror every day proud of what you see, then I can too." She became one of my biggest fans and still is today. When people ask her about it, Debby says, "My sister empowered a lot of women to explore their bodies, their sexuality, and gain confidence in the bedroom. I look at all of the positive contributions that she's made." I like that.

As for my mother finding out, well, I didn't find out how she came to know my secret until 2009 when we reconnected and talked about it for the first time. Mom told me, "Debby told me right away. She was a tattletale too like you were as a young girl. I was shocked but also happy that you were doing well. It was mixed. I always wanted my daughters to be very strong, on top of the world, and taking good care of themselves, and both of my daughters are. I'm proud."

CHAPTER 10

A Star Is Porn

With my New Year's resolution of taking it to the next level still fresh in mind, I marched into Digital Playground's offices on January 2, 2000, to talk business. I thought I was just there to talk, but Samantha Lewis, the co-owner of the company and my soon-to-be manager, had already prepared a contract for me and in my excitement, I did the unthinkable. I signed the contract without reading it, without having an attorney read it, and without knowing what the hell to say yes to and what to say no to. I blindly signed on the dotted line.

WHEN SIGNING A PORN CONTRACT . . .

Don't sign it without an attorney reading it first

Don't be drunk when you sign it

Don't forget to trademark your name before you enter into any business agreements

Don't let someone else own your website

Don't agree to "air tight" (air tight means a dick in your mouth, pussy, and ass at the same time)

Don't make less money than your manager

Don't let your management and production company be one and the same

Don't shoot more than one movie a month

Don't agree to arbitration if it comes to that

Don't sign anything that contains the phrases "in perpetuity" or "throughout the universe"

The negotiations weren't really negotiations at all. It went a little something like this:

Samantha asked, "How much do you need to live?"

"About five thousand a month," I stupidly replied. It seemed to be my magic number. I got $5,000 for *Penthouse* and $5,000 for *Virtual Sex*. "OK, that's what we'll pay you," Samantha was quick to agree. She was a bit too quick to agree and I found out later what a raw deal I signed.

"Great!" I was elated. I was now a contract girl. Sam, Ali, and I went out to Delmonico's Steak and Lobster House in Encino to celebrate. I dined on lobster and champagne and was on top of the world.

From that moment on, things started happening really fast, and I was becoming very close with Sam. She became like a big sister, or almost a mother figure for me. We'd talk every day, sometimes three, four, five times a day. We'd shop, go out to lunch, gossip, share beauty tips, hit the gym, and do all the things that close girl-friends do. She handled everything for me, such as my schedule, hiring the right makeup and hair people for my jobs, leasing me a car to drive, everything. Because she was older than me, I looked up to her and learned a lot about life from her. And I trusted her like you'd trust a close family member. And even Ali acted like a father figure to me.

"Guess what?" Samantha asked me. "You're going to AVN. You'll be signing at a booth. It'll be great." Signing at AVN really meant you made it. *Adult Video News* is the Bible of the porn industry. Every year in January, they have an awards show and convention in, appropriately enough, Sin City—Las Vegas. And all of the big stars would go and plug their new movies, meet their fans, sign autographs, and party.

I flew to Vegas about a week later and immediately hit the convention floor. I arrived at the booth in Vegas, and there was a stack of 8 × 10 glossy photos of me that said *Virtual Sex with Tera Patrick*. Two Sharpies sat next to the stack. And next to the Sharpies were Nikki Tyler and Julia Ann, who used to partner with Janine in *Blondage*, a dancing act they performed at strip clubs. And then there was this really loud, outgoing, beautiful woman named Teri Weigel.

"Hey!" Teri, dressed in nothing but a G-string and pasties, yelled to me. "You're the new girl! Awesome! Hi! I'm Teri! So nice to meet you!"

I was a little nervous going in, but my nerves immediately went away. The other girls didn't introduce themselves to me at first, so I latched onto the much friendlier Teri. She was a *Playboy* Playmate in 1987 and is the only Playmate to have gone into porn. I looked at her with awe. Here was this beautiful, powerful woman with a microphone in her hand, commanding a crowd of people to come on by. She stood on a chair, loud, confident, and gorgeous as hell.

I had no idea what the fuck I was doing, or if I'd even have any fans to sign those glossy photos for. But lo and behold, fans knew who I was and were coming to see me. It was the first time I met any of my fans, and I loved them immediately. I jumped right in and started signing "Tera Patrick" in my chicken scratch. I didn't know what or how to sign an autograph. I was thinking about how Marilyn Monroe signed her name.

I said to my new friend, "Hey, Teri, how do you sign an autograph?"

Teri Weigel

"Awww, sweetie. Here . . ." and she took a blank piece of paper out and proceeded to write my name in all different ways with different lines like "Love, Tera Patrick," "Love & Lust, Tera Patrick," "Fucking Fuck Me, Tera Patrick." She wrote out all of these little signatures and I started signing them one after another. When there wasn't a line of fans, I'd practice my signature on paper. My name was still new to me, so I wasn't used to signing it yet.

Teri took me under her wing. She taught me how to do my makeup for the bright lights at a signing like this. She taught me how to handle my fans. She basically taught me how to "do AVN" and how to be a porn celebrity.

"Girl, you are going to have this down and you are going to be a huge star," she told me after our long day of signing. I'll never forget her kindness, and I tried to be like Teri to the new girls that came into the business after I got more famous. There were times when I'd be bitchy to the new girls, but I'd catch myself and think, "Teri would be so disappointed in me if she knew I was being a bitch."

Things were happening fast with Digital Playground. They got me the Playboy TV gig on *Night Calls 411 Live* show next. It was a live, call-in television show where horny guys and gals phoned in their sex and relationship questions, talked about their fantasies, and interacted with the show's hosts, who would masturbate on air or demonstrate sex toys and other things like that. I went through a whole round of auditions and finally landed the role of the Net Nympho. Crystal Knight and Flower Edwards were the show's hosts, and they couldn't have a third host, so I became the Internet girl and I'd read e-mails from viewers, banter with them, and give a little striptease as I did my thing. I was the Net Nympho for the first year and then I became the cohost with Crystal Knight after Flower got pregnant and left in June 2001.

I loved being on TV, but I loved it a little too much. Every day was a party for me, and I was drinking more heavily than I ever had. I didn't do a single episode of *Night Calls* sober. Every night on the set, the production manager would come up to me and say, "All right, Stick"—they called me Stick because I was so thin at the time—"what's it going to be tonight?" And I'd name my drink of choice. I'd often get a fifth of Jack Daniel's and a two-liter bottle of Coke and it would either be half gone or entirely gone before the night's end.

I'm shocked I didn't get fired. I was smashed on every episode of that show. The director, Jeff, and my producer, Jamie, would have to give me direction in my earpiece to keep me alert. "Tera, your eyes are closed. Tera, open your eyes. Tera, sit up straight. Tera, put your shoulders back. Tera, Tera, Tera!" It was always something with me. But I was happy. I was becoming the biggest porn star out there. I was on TV; my webcam show, *The Tera Patrick Show,* in front of a live

Crystal Knight, my Night Calls *costar*

audience on TeraPatrick.com, was up and running and going strong; and I was just drinking out of celebration. Or so I thought at the time. I was a party girl and I wanted to party like a rock star.

Looking back on it now, it was a pretty depressing existence, but I wasn't aware of it in the moment. As far as I was concerned, I had accomplished my New Year's resolution and took it to the next level. I was going to be *Penthouse*'s February 2000 Pet of the Month. I became a *Hustler* Honey. Digital Playground was keeping me busy with photo shoots and lots of press—they even hired me a full-time publicist! I knew I had made the right decision. Something really good was happening here. I was getting my $5,000 a month from Digital, plus I was getting about $3,000 an episode for *Night Calls*, and I was shooting for all the magazines. I was bringing in about $20,000 a month.

And on top of that, I had my first experience of truly feeling like a star. Sam and I flew to France for the 2000 Hot d'Or adult film awards, which, at the time, were part of the Cannes Film Festival. I was there to win Best American New Starlet. When we got off the plane, I couldn't believe how many fans gathered at the airport to greet me with signs that read WELCOME TERA! and HELLO TERA! and TERA'S NO. 1 FAN! and WE LOVE YOU TERA! As if that wasn't overwhelming enough, when I got in the car to head to an interview, there were two police cars with sirens escorting us to the TV studio. I couldn't believe it. Only a year in the business, and I had a police escort!

My publicist looked to me and said, "Oh my goodness. It's like you are Demi Moore!"

I was loving it, but I was also turning into a spoiled brat. When Samantha showed me my *Penthouse* issue, she was bursting with excitement.

"I have a surprise for you!" she said excitedly, pulling the magazine out from her bag with pride.

I looked at the magazine and my first thought was, "I'm not on the cover."

Samantha was like, "Ta-da!"

"I'm not on the cover," was all I could say.

"But you're *Penthouse* Pet of the Month!" she said.

"I'm not on the cover." I was pissed.

Samantha explained to me the reason I wasn't on the cover was because the *Penthouse* Pet of the Year is always on the January cover and the runner up was always on the February cover. So, if you get Pet of the Month in January or February (I was the February Pet), you don't get the cover. But I got over it. I was so happy with the spread. It turned out really beautiful, so I called up Suze Randall and said, "Thank you for making me look so beautiful, Suze!" Suze said, "Oh, Popkins"—that's what she called me because it rhymed with my real last name, Hopkins—"you're the one that looks smashing. I didn't have to do anything, my little piggy. My little slut."

Sure enough, two years later in 2002, I landed *Penthouse* Pet of the Year Runner-Up and finally got on the cover of the magazine.

From my 2000
Penthouse *pictorial*

And around the same time, as fate would have it, I found myself with a new shot at *Playboy*, the magazine I *really* wanted to be in. This is what I wanted my entire life and it was finally happening. *Playboy* was doing a big porn-star special. I was officially a big porn star by then, and they wanted me to be part of it. We shot it in November 2001 for the March 2002 issue dubbed "The Women of Porn," featuring me, Kira Kener, and Dasha on the cover. And not on the cover, but inside, were Jenna Jameson, Taylor Hayes, Julia Ann, Chasey Lain, Lacey, Janine Lindemulder, Brittany Andrews, Juli Ashton, and Asia Carrera.

Jenna Jameson was clearly the biggest porn star in the room, but Janine and I were hot on her tail. I think most people at the shoot assumed it would be Jenna, Janine, and me landing the cover together, but that's not exactly how it turned out. The photographer was shooting us in all different configurations, and as I was being shot with Kira and Dasha, I had butterflies in my stomach hoping it would be *the* shot. Then I heard the editor, Marilyn Grabowski, say to an assistant,

"Oh, that's my shot." My manager, Samantha, kept telling me I would be on the cover, so I already had my hopes up for it. She was right.

Competition for the cover aside, the vibe on the set was very festive and exciting. Everyone got along great, and no one caused drama. The final shot of the day was the big group orgy shot where all twelve of us were stark-naked, lying on a big bed together with all of our arms and legs intertwined. They placed Jenna next to me and as we were figuring out how to pose together, Jenna said to me, "Wow, someone's got long legs. Life is so rough." I smirked, knowing I would be on the cover and she wouldn't and thought, "Yeah, now life really *is* rough. Ha!" There was always a friendly fake competition between Jenna and me. I always gathered that she was not happy knowing that I was on the rise.

The excitement of the day got the best of me, and I missed out

A Polaroid outtake from the shoot for Playboy's *"Women of Porn" issue*

The orgy shot

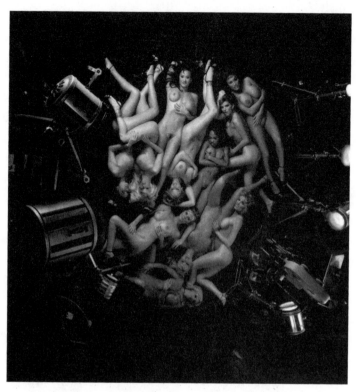

on my chance to tell Janine how much I loved her. I was such a huge fan of Janine's, but I was just too intimidated to talk to her. She had such a rock-star attitude and I knew she had dated Vince Neil and was famous for fucking famous musicians. I wanted to get some tips from her, but I was too afraid. She was such a goddess to me.

Even though my *Penthouse* cover was the February issue and my *Playboy* cover was the March issue, the two magazines overlapped a bit on the newsstands when they came out and it was the first time any woman was on the cover of both *Penthouse* and *Playboy* at the same time. It was quite an accomplishment for me. When *Playboy* came out, I ran down to my neighborhood newsstand on the corner of Ventura Boulevard and Van Nuys Boulevard in Sherman Oaks, and I lined up all the *Playboy* magazines and all the *Penthouse*

magazines that I was on the cover
of and just stared at them. Finally
someone said, "That's you!"

"Yes, it is!" I was so proud to say.

I was so proud, but my father
was even prouder. Before the magazines hit the newsstands, I decided
it was time to tell my father what I
was really up to. He was about to
figure it out soon enough when he
saw his daughter on the cover of
Playboy with a headline that read
SIZZLING PORN STAR PICTORIAL.

With Janine in 2001

I had started to talk to my fa-
ther again. Due to busy work schedules and living in different cities
or states over the years, we would sometimes not talk as much as
we should. But he came to visit me at my new place on Dickens
Street in Sherman Oaks, one of the nicer cities in the San Fernando
Valley, which was another upgrade in my living situation.

Like ripping off a Band-Aid, I told dad very quickly. I said, "Dad,
I've done some movies."

"Of course you have," he said very matter-of-fact.

There was a long pause. I was dumb and naïve to think that no
one watches porn or knew what I was up to. I told him that I was very
happy and that I was making a lot of money and that I was doing it
on my own terms. Then he said, "Will you sign a couple of these
Playboys for my friends?" I felt relieved. He was proud to see me on
the cover of *Playboy*. It was the approval I had been looking for my
whole life.

"It's an honor to be in *Playboy*, honey. I'm happy for you," he
said. "Just be careful. Take care of yourself, and be happy."

CHAPTER 11

Life Is a Porn Movie

As porn's It girl, I was getting my freak on when I wanted, where I wanted, and with whom I wanted. My favorite places to shoot and fuck were exotic, remote, faraway lands. Such was the scenario for the *Penthouse* video *Penthouse: Pets in Paradise,* which we filmed in tropical Costa Rica in 2001. *Penthouse* shoots were always so beautiful and tantalizing. This one was a softcore video with fellow porn stars and Pets Sunny Leone and Kyla Cole under the guidance of Nick Guccione, the son of the late great Bob Guccione, who founded *Penthouse.*

I was in heaven. I was trying to be professional and do my job, but all I wanted to do was have sex in this tropical paradise. It was frustrating for horny ol' me because the shoot was only softcore—just girl-on-girl scenes with no penetration. It was driving me crazy. But I had a plan to get some satisfaction. I had my eye on the brother of the photographer. He was a blond boy who looked like he was straight off the beaches of California.

During the day, I was shooting with the photographer—a brown-haired guy who was kind of geeky and not exactly my type. We were shooting on an active volcano in the middle of nowhere, with monkeys swinging from tree to tree and the biggest bugs I've ever seen in all my life. (I was the perfect porn star to bring into the great outdoors because I grew up hiking, camping, and hunting with my father. I loved being outside.)

So the photographer was shooting me and he kept backing up and backing up farther and farther to get the right angle until finally the mountain gave way and his leg buckled and fell through a hole with hot lava underneath. Everyone freaked out. The shoot stopped. Selfish me was bummed that I had to stop shooting for the day. Nick Guccione and the photographer's brother had to carry the burn victim off the mountain. He then had to get airlifted to the nearest hospital to be treated for second-degree burns on his leg.

Later on at dinner, we all feasted on fresh fruit, vegetables, and fish in the common dining area of the resort we were staying at, and the photographer excused himself from dinner because he wasn't feeling well. He was bandaged up from ankle to calf and the doctors had him medicated. I was slowly nursing my glass of white wine and getting a little buzzed and started thinking, "Hmmm. I think he needs a little attention. He's had a rough day." So being the horny girl that I am who loves to get fucked in gorgeous green surroundings like this one, I decided to follow the photographer to his room and make my move on him.

Knock! Knock!

"Come in," he said.

Shocked at the sight of me standing in his doorway he said, "What are you doing here?

"I thought you might need a little resuscitation," I said in my best porn-star voice. I loved using cheesy lines on guys like that— life was a porn movie to me.

He was lying in bed with his bandaged leg out of the covers and I slowly started to kiss him and took my panties off. I took his hand and put it on my wet pussy. He got hard instantly. I gently started taking his clothes off. I used to be a nurse, so in my mind I was pretending I was a super sexy nurse taking care of a patient. I was very gentle with him because I knew he was in a lot of pain and wouldn't be able to do much. I did all the work. I climbed on top of him and used him like the sex kitten that I was.

"Wow. I'm having sex with a *Penthouse* Pet," he told me.

We had sex for fifteen to twenty minutes before his brother busted in the door. It so happened that they were sharing a room. With the photographer's cock still inside of me, I turned around when I heard the brother come through the door and I said, "Ooh! Double time!"

"Whoa. What's going on in here? Is there a party?" the brother, who was a little drunk, slurred.

"Yeah, there's a party and you're invited!" I loved playing the porn star.

"No, no, no. You have to leave," said his brother, lying there under me.

"No, I want you both to stay," I insisted. The laid-up brother was not too pleased at my idea. But I had never had brothers before and I wanted them both, so I had them both.

I climbed off the photographer and started giving the blond brother a little mouth-to-mouth resuscitation. We started playing together and I gave him head. The blond brother had a bigger cock, so I was really excited. But the oral sex was too much for him to handle and he came all over my tits before we could fuck. I went back to the brother in bed and tried to finish my job there, but between being interrupted by his brother and being in pain from his injured leg, the photographer never got off. And he was not happy. It kind of ruined the moment for him. I felt bad.

The next morning, the blond brother came down to breakfast all bright and cheery saying, "What a fabulous morning it is!"

"Oh yes. I slept great," I said with a wink.

The brunette brother just grunted.

Oh well, you can't please everyone. But I certainly pleased myself.

My Tips for a Happy Threesome:

Here are a few tips on how to make sure a threesome goes your way and everyone is happy.

TIP 1: The girl is always in charge. We're the ones more likely to get jealous or feel uneasy, so the girl should be the one who lays out how it's going to go down.

TIP 2: Definitely set up some ground rules. Spell out what is off limits, if anything, and what is fair game ahead of time so there are no surprises.

TIP 3: Never spend too much time with one sexual partner over the other. That's how fights break out. Give equal attention to each person in the room.

TIP 4: Don't do a threesome with a friend or close business associate. Pick a partner who is somebody you're never going to see again. If this person is already in your life and is going to pop up again and again, it can get uncomfortable for you.

CHAPTER 12

Four Reasons

In late 2000, I started dating singer/rapper Erik Schrody, better known as Everlast, the former singer of the hip-hop group House of Pain, which had a big hit in the early '90s with a song called "Jump Around." As a solo artist, he was pretty successful too, having hit number 1 with his song "What It's Like" in 1998, just a few years before I met him on the set of his music video for "I Can't Move" from his second solo album.

My agent called me one day with an opportunity to audition for his music video, and I knew a little bit about Everlast, who I called by his real name, Erik. But to me, it was just another job and just another good opportunity to do my thing, make some money, and have a bit of fun. Meeting him was such a clichéd Hollywood moment. Here I am the "hot girl in the video," and the star asked me to come to his trailer. So in my sheer black dress, with no panties on, I went waltzing into his trailer and was greeted with a big cloud of marijuana smoke and Erik standing there with three of his homeys, whom he immediately dismissed. I'm thinking, "Oh, no, is he going to pounce on me?"

"Hey, how's it going?" asked Erik while rolling a joint.

I was instantly attracted to him. The shaved head, tattoos, and tough-guy manner . . . I dug it.

"Do you want to smoke?"

"No, that's OK." I didn't smoke much during this time of my life.

"Well, uh, see you on set," he said. He was kind of cold, but it was intriguing for me. A challenge, I thought.

At the end of the shoot, he asked me for my number, which made me as giddy as a schoolgirl. I hadn't been dating much in the past few years because I just wasn't into having a boyfriend. I was into fucking, and something in Erik made me excited for a new adventure.

Our first date was a movie date at his house. Ladies, don't ever let a guy take you on a date to his *house*: (a) It's cheap, (b) It shows disrespect (What? He didn't want to be seen with me in public?), (c) It usually means all he wants from you is sex, and (d) It's just plain lame. We deserve dinners and romance, don't we? I should've known how lame Erik would end up being by that very first date. But I was young and naïve and just happy to have met a guy who could potentially be a boyfriend, which is something that had been lacking in my life.

I went to his house in Reseda, California, for that date, and it was really uncomfortable at first. We sat on opposite sides of his couch as we watched a Lakers game, which had me bored out of my mind. We both seemed really nervous. After a few awkward moments, he took a thick, fuzzy fur blanket and wrapped me in it and then wrapped himself in it. I was cold and shivering, partly because it was winter and pretty chilly in his house and partly because I was a little nervous. Either way, he warmed me up fast. And unbeknownst to me at the time, we started a pattern that would be the basis of our relationship: I come to his house. We sit on his couch. We watch TV. We have sex. I go home, utterly unsatisfied.

For two years, I'd follow that pattern. The sex was never mind-blowing. You can tell if sex is going to be good by how much effort a guy puts into you when you're not under the sheets. Erik put zero effort into dating me, taking me out, or making me feel special or beautiful, and that selfishness extended into the bedroom. He was very selfish, but I just went along because it was nice to have someone new around. I had been really lonely, and it was a time when I was feeling really low.

Along the way during those two years, he'd say things to me like, "You know, you're lucky to be with me. Who's going to want to date a porn chick?" Well, *he* was dating a porn chick, so what the fuck? He was clearly torn over dating me. On the one hand, he's saying no one should date a porn chick. On the other hand, he's asking me to autograph my *Penthouse* cover. What was that? And the worst part about it was that he asked me to sign the *Penthouse* right after we had sex. Two words: tacky and creepy. He was attracted to what I did for a living but repelled by it at the same time. And it felt like he punished me for being who I was.

I just remember thinking, "Well, it's bad enough that he doesn't love me for me. But it's worse that he seems to actually hate me for me." I wasn't really sure what to do with that, so I just let it slide for a while. But deep down, I felt hurt, humiliated, and depressed that the guy I had been with for about two years was treating me so badly, and I was letting him. It was also sad that he lived with his mother, but his mother never spoke to me and we never interacted. Erik obviously kept it that way on purpose.

During this time I had very low self-esteem and was drinking heavily, and Erik's comments just dragged me down further. A low point in the relationship came on my birthday. In general, 2002 was a banner year for me. I landed both *Playboy* and *Penthouse*. I was one of the hosts of Playboy TV's *Night Calls 411 Live* and I was enjoying the press and promotion of the two simultaneous covers. Everyone was celebrating me around me, but deep down I was very depressed and felt so alone. Being with Erik made me even lonelier than being by myself because he wasn't there for me, supporting me, loving me, or respecting me.

July 25, 2002, was my twenty-sixth birthday. I called up Erik and said, "Hey, it's my birthday! What are we doing?

And he said, "I don't know what you're doing, but I'm going out with the boys."

"You're not taking me out?" I asked.

"Why would I fucking take you out? You can do whatever the fuck you want to do," Erik said.

I shouldn't have been surprised at his reaction, but I was, and I cried and cried and cried.

I called my best friend, Alexis Winston, who was a *Penthouse* Pet and dating a millionaire named Larry, and told her how sad and depressed I was and she came up with a plan. "Forget about Erik. I'm going to take you on Larry's private jet and we're going to get away." So I packed my bag, got dolled up, and flew up to central California with Alexis and her man, who had a big birthday cake waiting for me. I was so jealous of her relationship. When I got to Larry's mansion all I could think was, "Wow. He's going to marry her and she gets to live in this thirty-room house with the man of her dreams and here I am dating shitty, selfish asshole Erik. What am I doing wrong?"

Erik did such a number on my self-esteem that I started to cry myself to sleep at night thinking, "What man is ever going to marry a porn star? Maybe Erik's right. Who is going to want to bring me home to their parents?" Seeing Alexis so happy with her man and all of these girls in the industry around me dating guys who lavished love and gifts on them made me really think about what I wanted in life. I wanted to marry a good man. And if porn was going to get in the way of that, I though, then maybe I shouldn't do porn anymore.

Around this time we were shooting *Island Fever 2* for Digital Playground in a rain forest in Hawaii. Perfect, a tropical setting, my favorite. It ended up being my worst filming experience ever. I was working with a Canadian porn actor named Erik Everhard, whom I worked with before on a *Penthouse* photo shoot with Suze, on the movie *White*

From Island Fever 2

Panty Chronicles and many other things over the years. I remember him being a genuinely nice guy when I first worked with him.

I was in cowgirl position on top of him, and all of a sudden something in him snapped. He started fucking me violently, so hard that I bled everywhere. He actually tore my vagina. It was embarrassing and violating. I didn't even realize I was bleeding; I just knew that he was pounding the shit out of me and it hurt. I was so tired of working at this point that I just shut off my emotions, turned that "switch" on, and went through with my job. The director saw the blood and stopped the scene. He had to take me off the set. I wasn't able to work for the rest of the movie. I had other scenes planned but was only able to shoot this one scene. It was a horrible experience. He didn't even apologize. No one there even comforted me. There's no comforting in porn, I guess.

I went back to my room that day and thought, "Wow. Is McDonald's hiring?" It left such a bitter taste in my mouth. This was not what I signed up for. For a split second, I thought, "I don't want to do movies anymore. I just don't want to do it." I loved having sex, but this episode left me feeling violated and used. However, I felt like I was in too deep and I couldn't quit even if I wanted to. It's who I was, and I didn't want to lose all that I had built up over the years. I didn't want to lose my fans. I didn't want to lose my livelihood. And my "boyfriend" Erik had me convinced that I was just some stupid porn chick who couldn't do anything else. What was I going to do if I quit? So, I didn't. Not yet.

I started sinking lower and hitting the bottle extra hard. Up until this point, I drank with a party-girl attitude. It was celebratory drinking because life was indeed going pretty damn well. But eventually I was drinking myself to bed every night and needing booze to get through *Night Calls*. I was lonely and I wanted a good man to be with. I never regretted what I did for a living because it was always my choice, my way, my fantasies lived out. But the outside factors were starting to take their toll on me.

My lowest moment during what was supposed to be this "stellar year" for me came on the set of *Night Calls* one random evening. I had downed a fifth of Jack Daniel's and could barely stand. I don't remember much from the night, but I do remember that R&B singer Brian McKnight was in the studio audience watching the show. We'd often have celebrities pop by to watch us tape and I always had fun interacting with them, but not that night.

"Are you OK?" Crystal Knight, my cohost, asked repeatedly. Crystal really looked out for me. She could tell by the glazed-over look in my eyes that something was way wrong.

"No. I'm not OK. I don't think I can do the show," I told her.

"You can do the show. I'll carry you. Don't worry. I'll do all the work," she assured me. She had my back. She knew I'd get fired if I couldn't do the show because I was too drunk.

I was making it through the shoot, but my condition didn't go entirely unnoticed. My producer Jamie kept saying in my earpiece,

"Stick! What's wrong with you? Wake up!" My eyes had been rolling back into my head. I couldn't believe how wasted I was.

It was then that I realized how fucked-up I was getting, and how I was about to fuck up my career and life if I didn't get myself together. I was drinking myself to sleep every night, having bad hangovers, feeling like crap, acting cranky to people around me, and starting to fuck up at work—the one thing that I loved. After that bad night on the *Night Calls* set, I vowed to take some time off from drinking, but it wasn't easy or immediate.

There was also the money issue. Here I was the most famous porn star in the world, and I was still living in a small condo and driving a leased Infiniti that I would later find out was in my manager's name, not mine. I just wasn't making the money I thought I should be making. I was making about $20,000 a month between all of my gigs, and that sounds like a lot, but in the porn industry it isn't. It's a lot of money in comparison to a civilian lifestyle, but not for an entertainer. Most actresses make a lot more than just a quarter of a million a year. And the number-one porn star in the world is only making $240,000? Bankers make more than that! People thought I would be driving a Rolls-Royce, and I wasn't. I started seeing girls in the industry making a ton more money, wearing fancier designer clothes, and driving more expensive luxury cars. I had none of that, and I didn't understand why.

I just wasn't reaping the benefits of working as hard as I did. I always had money to pay my bills, but not as much as I should have. Erik was the one who started me getting suspicious of my situation. He said, "You know, your manager is driving a brand-new Mercedes and a brand-new Denali and she dresses really well and lives in this huge mansion and is always taking vacations. And you rent this condo. Your manager shouldn't be making more than you do." That was a big wake-up call for me.

One day, I called my manager Samantha and I told her, "Listen, I want to have lunch and there's some things I want to get off my chest." She agreed that it was time for a serious talk. She clearly had things to get off her chest too.

I'll admit it. I was becoming difficult to work with and was growing angry toward her and Digital Playground. I was showing up to work on time and never looking like a hag or anything, but I was bitchy and becoming difficult and demanding. I'd be like, "Fuck you all. I fucking hate you. I need a drink. I'm not going on until you bring me a fucking Coke. I don't want this makeup artist, I want that one." And on and on I'd go. I turned into a full-blown diva.

It wasn't just about the money. We were growing apart, and I wanted more out of life. I wanted a fuller life—a real relationship with a good guy, a social life, and, yeah, a nicer house and nicer car. It was always work, work, work, work, work. I was overworked, underpaid, stressed out, and exhausted. There was always a store signing or an appearance or a shoot or an interview. The schedule was too much. I was Digital Playground's only contract girl between 1999 and 2002. I was the face of Digital Playground, so all of the promotion fell on my tired shoulders. It was "Tera, we need you in Minneapolis. Tera, we need you in Europe."

I appreciated the work for a while, of course, but it was taking its toll on me, and I wasn't taking care of myself. It was a battle with my manager and production company, but it was also a battle with myself. I was drinking heavily to mask my true feelings, which were loneliness, pain, depression, and sadness. And underneath it all was this hunger for love and a deep connection with someone. I just wanted to be loved and have someone to love, and at the time I didn't know if staying in porn and working at the pace I was working at would get me to that goal.

At the end of *Night Calls* on Wednesday nights, there'd be a social gathering at a bar or on the set to celebrate. Instead of participating, I would drink alone in my dressing room, get in my car, drive home drunk, and then drink more at home by myself. I was becoming very antisocial and experiencing a lot of highs and lows.

On the days I was feeling high, I'd shop like crazy, spend what money I had, and fuck my neighbor, a grip on a shoot, or sometimes even Erik. And on the days I was low, I'd sleep for twelve hours, not answer the phone, watch MTV2 for hours on end, drink my Jack and Coke or wine coolers or gin and tonic, and pass out.

At our lunch meeting I basically told my manager Sam, "Look, I've been acting the way I'm acting because I'm not happy and I want a break." She agreed that I needed a break. I was clearly miserable with my life, my relationship, and my work, and I was drinking way too much. It was obvious that I needed some time off to get my shit together. And I started to not enjoy the sex as much as I used to. It became harder to orgasm, because I was just unhappy in my contract and stressed out. And that's no fun. That's why I got into porn in the first place.

My plan was this: Take a hiatus from porn. Get sober. Figure out why I didn't have a lot of money and where my money was going. And let the fog I was in lift a bit to get some clarity. I had no idea what I was going to do beyond that, but I knew I wanted to have a more normal life. I knew I needed to work on my self-esteem and work on myself, but I just didn't know how.

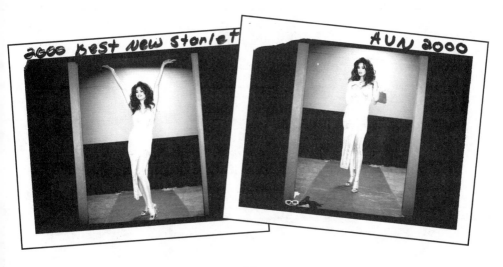

CHAPTER 13

When Tera Met Evan

As they say, timing is everything. I believe I met Evan at the perfect time in my life, but it almost didn't happen that way. In the late '90s my best friend was a Swedish lady named Anneli Adolfsson. She came to America when she was twenty years old to be a rock-and-roll and porn photographer. And she became very successful in her field. One of the first rock stars she ever photographed was Evan Seinfeld, lead singer and bassist of the hardcore rock band Biohazard. Evan also would play a badass biker on HBO's prison drama *Oz*.

Anneli and Evan had known each other for a long time, and she used to hang out with the band and a lot of the other hardcore bands that Evan was friends with. They basically ran in the same rock-and-roll circle.

One day, she and I were having a fun chick day in good old Sherman Oaks. We were getting our nails done, having lunch, and gossiping as girls do. Halfway through our lunch, she said to me, "I want to introduce you to this guy Evan Seinfeld, and I want to shoot you for his band's album cover."

I asked her, "Who are we talking about? What band is he in?"

"Biohazard. They're an awesome hardcore band," she said.

"Who the fuck is Biohazard?" I was such a snob about it. "Let me know when I can be on a Metallica album cover." I was a little too cool for school about the whole thing. When I was fourteen I was hanging out at a club in Japan with Guns N' Roses, and now she wanted me to do some photo shoot with a band I'd never heard of? No thanks.

I totally dismissed it, and didn't even bother to lock the name, Evan Seinfeld, in my mind.

Fast-forward to the year 2002 when I was at the tail end of dating Erik. I would look into Erik's eyes and just not see any sparkle, and certainly not see any love for me. He never told me I was pretty, he never wined and dined me, and he never made me feel good about myself. There was no purpose to it.

One Sunday night, Erik and I were hanging out at his place, watching HBO's *Oz*. I'd never seen it before. I looked up at the TV screen and I saw a naked, tattooed man run across the screen with his penis swinging in all its glory. This naked man was so hot and he had this strong, powerful voice. He really struck me because he had looked so bad, so strong and dangerous. He was exactly what I had always wanted in a man. He was totally unlike any guy I had ever dated before, and he was the complete opposite of the guy sitting on the couch next to me. I thought I was getting a tattooed badass when I met Erik, but he was not the real deal. In this naked man on the screen, though, I saw a nice guy with a tough-guy exterior. I instantly thought to myself, "That dark figure who's running across the screen with a big wiener is going to be my husband someday."

My relationship with Erik was over at that moment.

Erik was also excited by the sight of this man, but for a different reason. They knew each other.

"Hey, Tera. Look, it's my boy Evan!"

"Oh, really. Evan who?"

"Evan Seinfeld. He's from the band Biohazard."

It still didn't click in my head that my photographer friend Anneli tried to get us together a few years earlier. But I was intrigued. I kept the name Evan Seinfeld in my head and I started calling around to everyone I knew to see if anyone knew how I could get in touch with this man. It became this "Where's Waldo?" kind of search where everyone seemed to know who he was, but couldn't give me any real leads on how to get in touch with him. Remember, this was before the days of Facebook, MySpace, and Twitter, where everyone is easy to find at the click of a mouse.

So, I called my friend Paul who worked in the television business. I figured since he worked in the TV industry, maybe he could help me out. He said, "Are you kidding me? You want to meet that guy Evan Seinfeld from *Oz*?"

"Yeah, I'm really interested in meeting him. He's really hot," I replied. Paul clearly wasn't happy. He said, "I don't want you to meet Evan Seinfeld. He would be bad for you. He would make you his cock puppet." But that just piqued my interest even more. If this hot, tattooed, strong-looking man with the big dick wanted to make me his cock puppet, that would be fine with me!

Paul suggested I call up HBO to try to get ahold of Evan. He gave me a number to call, and I did. But I didn't get anywhere. I was transferred from department to department until someone finally spoke to me.

"Don't hang up!" I screamed, probably sounding crazy and desperate.

"I'm looking for one of your actors," I told the lady on the phone.

"Are you a reporter?" she asked.

"No."

"Well, who are you with?"

"No one. It's a personal call."

Silence.

"His name is Evan Seinfeld and he's on *Oz* and I know this may sound strange, but I'd like to give you my name and number so you can pass it along to him."

More silence.

I had been put on hold and transferred so many times that I just sat there and waited, thinking she was actually helping me out. A minute went by and I was like, "Hello? Hello? Are you there?"

She had hung up on me.

A few days later I was chatting with my friend Anneli, still not making the connection that she had already tried to introduce me to Evan. I said to her, "Hey, Anneli, you know a lot of musician types. Do you know this guy Evan Seinfeld from Biohazard?" By that time I had searched for Evan on the Internet to find out more about him. "I saw him on *Oz* and he's super hot and I'm really interested in him."

And then there was yet more silence on the other end of the phone. Finally, I heard, "Ahem. I tried to introduce you to him years ago."

"Oh my God! That's the guy you wanted me to do a photo shoot with?!"

"Yeah, yeah. See how well I know your type?"

But then she added, "Careful, Tera. I know I tried to set you two up, but he does have a reputation with the ladies."

"Well, I still want to meet him. He looks really good naked," I replied.

She told me, "Well, I'll tell you what. I'll call him and I'll give him your number, and we'll see where it goes from there."

What I didn't know at the time was that she called him up immediately after our conversation and told him the following: "My best friend Tera wants to meet you. She's a good girl and if you screw her over, I'll totally kill you." He was like, "Tera who?" So she made him get online and Google my name and he did. Then he said to her, "What is wrong with this girl? She's gorgeous. She wants to go out with me?"

She gave Evan my number and a few days later he called. It was late in the afternoon and I picked up the phone and I heard his voice, "Hi, this is Evan. Is this Tera?"

I quickly turned down the volume on the music I was listening to, because I wanted to hear his voice better. I got butterflies in my stomach, and said in a sexy voice, "I'm so glad you called." He sounded cautious on the phone. Not me. I was the forward one, which I would soon find out was quite the opposite of how things usually were. He was the one calling chicks and putting his cards on the table. And at this time in my life, I was the shy one. Being an adult film star, I wasn't the type who would put it out there, because guys expect me to be swinging from the chandeliers. So I usually had to hold it back, but I didn't with Evan. I wanted to swing from the chandeliers with him right away.

On that first call we talked for hours. We talked about everything. He told me about his son, about the music business, and about his life. He told me that he had seen my picture and that he thought I was beautiful, but he didn't come off as creepy as so many men do when they say, "I've seen your photos and I think you're hot." I loved the sound of his voice. He sounded like a tough, strong, and confident man. I hung on every word he said about growing up on the wrong side of Brooklyn in a Jewish family and living around real New York mobsters.

I immediately felt close to him. We connected on a deep level because we had similar upbringings and life stories. We both left our families at an early age and started our lives and careers in our teen years. He grew up on the streets of Brooklyn and I on the streets of fashion in Tokyo. We had both been to the school of hard knocks and learned about life the hard way. And neither of us was close to our families at the time.

We were both lonely. A lot of people loved us and adored us, but it was from afar. He had music fans and groupies and I had perverted guys who fantasized about me. But neither of us had anyone who loved or adored us for who we were outside of our careers. We met at a time when we both longed for something deeper, more meaningful. For once in my life, I didn't see him as a guy who could just satisfy me sexually, but as a man who could fill my heart and satisfy my emotional needs as well.

I went into work that night full of excitement about Evan. I told all of my friends on set, "He called me! He fucking called!" I had been driving everyone crazy for weeks leading up to that call, especially Crystal, and she wanted to hear all about it. Jamie, our producer, was just like, "OK, Stick. Get onstage now." It was a big deal. Everyone was rooting for me. No one had liked me being with Erik, so they were excited that I was excited about someone.

I came home from work that night and immediately called Evan back and we talked for about two hours. I could tell that he would be what I wanted. And what I wanted was for a man to take control. I'm more submissive, and I like it that way. I knew he would be the yin to my yang. And every night that week we talked on the phone. It was an amazing, romantic courtship, made even more tantalizing and exciting by the fact that we'd never even been in the same room.

Our relationship took off from there. Starting with that first phone call in May 2002, we talked on the phone every night. We talked about everything: music, art, history, you name it. We had long, deep, soulful conversations about life, and it really took me to a whole other level of intimacy. I couldn't stop thinking about him. I would look at his picture and fantasize about him and wonder what it was like to actually be with him.

We decided not to meet in person until both of our shows wrapped. He was shooting *Oz* during the week and had his son, Sammy, on weekends and was working on a new Biohazard album. And I was shooting *Night Calls* on Wednesdays and doing photo shoots, signings, or content for my webcast, *The Tera Patrick Show,* on weekends. So for three months, all we did was talk (and have our fair share of phone sex!). But it was the long talks that made me fall in love with him. For the first time, I took the time to get to know a man emotionally, intellectually, and spiritually before bonding with him physically. The three months apart forced me to get to know him and fall in love with who he was instead of letting my hormones take over and bonding over sex. I never took the time to connect with a man like I did with Evan. That's why it was so different.

There was so much that I loved about Evan, especially how he was such a good father to Sammy. He was so devoted to his son. He would talk about him for hours. I felt relieved that he already had a kid because I didn't want to have children. I was afraid I would abuse my child because my mother had abused me. I didn't want to repeat the pattern. I knew we were getting serious, and it was a relief that he already had the chance to be a father and wouldn't want or expect that from me if we took it to the next level.

Since I was going through a hard time when I first started talking to Evan, I initially didn't want him to know about my problems. So I told him that I was taking a break from porn because I just needed a rest. But I didn't tell him right away how unhappy I really was with my manager and Digital Playground or how much I was drinking. It was soon hard to hide my woes. Evan could tell right away that something was wrong. He's a recovering drug addict and has been sober for twenty years, so he saw the signs of my alcohol abuse right away. There would be nights when he'd call me at our scheduled ten p.m. time and I wouldn't answer. Mind you, it was ten p.m. my time in L.A., which was one a.m. his time in Brooklyn. It was sweet of him to stay up and call me at a time that was convenient for me. When I didn't pick up at ten, he'd call back at eleven and then at midnight and when I finally answered he'd say, "You've been drinking, haven't you?" Of course the answer was yes. I didn't pick up the phone because I was either passed out or throwing up or just didn't want him to hear me wasted.

Evan was the first man to be real with me and call me on my shit. He made me take a good, long, hard look at myself for the first time in my life and face my demons head-on instead of burying them or running away from them. He wouldn't let me get away with saying, "I'm fine. Nothing is wrong. Life is great." At that time, life wasn't great and I wasn't fine. And Evan knew it and wanted to help me through it.

If it weren't for Evan calling me out on my problems, I don't think I would've had the courage to admit them to myself. I finally admitted that I did need to shape up, and I started confiding in him about my troubles. For the first time, I had a real sounding board in my life who could give me strong, solid advice or at least help me get to a place where I could figure things out for myself.

Evan would ask me, "Why are you unhappy?"

At first, I'd put on a fake, happy front and say, "What? Me? I'm totally happy. Everything is great."

"No, everything is not great and you are not happy. You're drinking too much and you're obviously in a lot of emotional stress. And you wouldn't quit a career you loved if something wasn't really wrong there," Evan would say.

I finally let him in and let him help me. We talked at length about my situation with my money, my deal with Digital Playground, my family issues, and my drinking. And no matter how low I was, he was always there to talk me through any problem. He helped me feel good about myself. Underneath all the tattoos was just a nice Jewish boy from Brooklyn.

EVAN SEINFELD

Tera and I started our three-month courtship over the phone in May 2002. I had seen some pictures of her in *Playboy* and other magazines and I looked her up online. But I hadn't watched any of her movies. I wasn't that into porn at that point. I mean, I had always watched porn but I wasn't a fanatic who knew all the girls' names and everything about them. And even though I was falling in love with this girl on the phone, I couldn't help but think about what my boys back in Brooklyn thought about girls like that.

I grew up in that tough-guy Brooklyn way where you wanted respect and your girlfriend was supposed to be a virgin. It's that typical Jewish and Italian way of thinking. Your girl should be a virgin, but a slut with you behind closed doors. If someone in my neighborhood dated a girl who fucked a bunch of guys, she was considered a whore and a slut. And you couldn't be proud to bring her around. I don't agree with that way of thinking, but I couldn't help but have it on my mind.

I never set out to fall in love with a porn star. It just happened. My only fear in meeting Tera was wondering if I would measure up below the belt. I thought, "Oh my God. She had sex with professional guys who get paid to fuck who have really big dicks." Now, I know my dick is big. Girls have told me so. Lots of girls. But I did have to wonder if it was big compared to what she was used to. That was the one thing I was afraid of. I wasn't afraid that I was falling in love with a porn star. But I did wonder, "What if I'm in love with her but then I can't deal with what she does?" I thought I could handle it, but I couldn't help but fear that I might end up feeling like, "Why did I have to fall in love with you?"

The night before I was supposed to fly to California to meet Tera for the first time, I randomly ran into Jenna Jameson backstage at Korn's show at Hammerstein Ballroom in New York City. I knew who Jenna was, of course. And I had been introduced to her before. I have to say, I wasn't impressed. She used to be really cute. But here she was with no makeup on, bad skin, visible hair extensions, and she was wearing stretchy pants that had a hole in the butt.

So I'm talking to her and I politely tell her that I'm a fan, even though I really wasn't, and she tells me that she likes Biohazard. I believe her because she's friends with lots of rockers.

We're chitchatting and everything's cool. She had this weird guy with her who was wearing this *Cat in the Hat* hat and sporting scraggly dreads and tiny purple sunglasses. He looked like a douchebag and followed her around like a puppy. She kept shooing him away as she sat on the lap of David Draiman from the band Disturbed. I was totally creeped out by the guy. I asked Jenna who he was. And she goes, "Oh, that's just Jay. Don't mind him." Later, I find out Jay is her husband. I thought, "I hope I never hear the words 'Oh, that's just Evan. Don't mind him' out of the mouth of someone I'm with."

She asks me, "Don't you date some girls in the business?"

"Nope. I don't, actually. But funny you mention it because I've been talking on the phone with Tera Patrick for months and I think we're falling in love. I'm flying out tonight to see her." I don't normally share like that, but I was all goofy and in love. I never talked about a girl like I did with Tera. That's not like me. But Tera was different.

Jenna sighs. "Ugh. Tera Patrick." It sounded as if she was sick of hearing her name. And then Jenna goes, "Ewwww," and tries to change the subject immediately.

I'm like, "Wait. What? Tera is gorgeous."

Jenna takes another dramatic deep breath and replies, "She's kind of big."

"Huh?" She is so skinny, I'm thinking.

"Yeah. She's kind of big, loose, and jiggly."

Now, if I have a female phobia, it's "big, loose, and jiggly." Jenna Jameson's catty little comment struck a nerve through my fucking heart. She could've said "cracked out, diseased, and ugly," and it wouldn't have bothered me as much. Something deep inside me was shaken, not stirred. Here I was convinced that I was flying out to meet this girl who was once hot, but who's now "big, loose, and jiggly." I know I shouldn't have cared, but it's my one pet peeve. Here's where I'm coming from. If I'm standing at the bar with two girls and one girl is an 8 with a face like an angel but overweight and the other girl is a 5 with a hot little body, I'm taking the 5 with the hot body home because you can dim the lights. I can fuck a girl who's ugly; just turn her around and dim the lights. I can fuck average chicks. But the one thing I can't fuck is "big, loose, and jiggly."

My heart dropped to the pit of my stomach. I briefly considered not going to L.A. But then I looked over at Jenna and realized the source. Jenna wasn't looking that hot and Tera's star was on the rise. It was obvious she was just being a bitch. And besides, every picture I saw of Tera was stunning and I was falling in love with her and she with me.

I got on the plane, but I couldn't get the fear of the unknown out of my head. I somehow convinced myself that Tera was really just some ditzy porn chick and that even though we'd had all these great conversations, everything out of her mouth must have been a lie. Part of it was self-loathing. Here's this girl who can go out with any A-list celebrity or billionaire she wants and she likes me? Something must be wrong with her. To make myself feel better I made backup plans. To this day, Tera gives me shit about this. I had three separate backup plans with friends, and even one exgirlfriend, who I'd go see if Jenna was right.

Sherman Oaks Castle Park 3/1/2002

CHAPTER 14

The First Date

We finally made a date for September 4, 2002. The night before he was to fly across country, we stayed up on the phone for hours. He would fly into Long Beach Airport, arriving at seven o'clock in the morning and I'd be there to pick him up. I was really nervous about meeting him. But most of all, I couldn't stop thinking, "Is he going to like me?" And as great as our conversations had been on the phone, I was also a little worried about some of the things I'd heard about him from my friends. The words "pig," "womanizer," and "cock puppet" kept coming up. "Cock puppet" I liked. But what worried me was whether he really was a womanizing pig. In my heart, I knew from our hours on the phone that he was a good guy, but my head was trying to talk me out of it.

When I pulled over to pick him up, he was wearing his grandfather's fedora, shorts, and a sweatshirt. He looked very classy. He put down his small suitcase and took the toothpick out of his mouth, smiled, and said, "Well, it's really nice to meet you, Tera Patrick." I thought, "Yep, that's my husband. That is the smile I'm going to see when we're both ninety and gray."

I completely melted and felt weak all over. He put his hands on

Me and Evan on our first date

me, and when he touched my skin I felt this warm, intense feeling just building up inside of me—there was so much sexual tension. I had never in my entire life felt this way about anybody. His big hazel eyes were so alive, and I just wanted to stare into them forever.

He got in the car and he said, "Hi, Linda." I loved that he called me Linda. He saw me for who I really was. He'd flip between calling me Linda and Tera. Either was fine with me, really. And it was Linda he was meeting. I picked him up in nothing but a simple pair of Miss Sixty jeans and a white tank top, with my hair brushed straight and little makeup on and diamond studs in my ears. I wanted him to see the real me—pure and natural and not all porno-ed out. I wanted him to love me.

I can't remember our first kiss. But I remember our first sniff. He got in the car, leaned in really close, and smelled my neck and my hair. He gave me goose bumps. He touched my neck very gently and I got nervous. He said, "Wow. You are so beautiful." He just kept touching my hair and saying sweet things to me and I just kept thinking, "This is real."

We raced back home to my apartment in Sherman Oaks and couldn't wait to have sex. We walked in, he dropped his bags on the floor, and he took me by the hand and twirled me around to get a good look at me. And then he kissed me. This would be the first time of a zillion times he would take me by the hand and spin me around. It became our special little thing. After that tender moment, we couldn't help but rip each other's clothes off. I finally got to see that big cock of his that I got a glimpse of on *Oz* and was happy to see that it was even bigger than I thought—nine inches and with good girth. We were trying to impress each other and outdo the other. We had a competitive vibe going, like "I'm a porn star." "Well, I'm a rock star." He thought he was the sexual dynamo, and I knew I was the sex bomb. We literally tried to outfuck each other, doing all of these crazy things to impress the other. "Yeah, you like that? Well, take *this*!" Or, "You like doggy-style? I'll do doggy-style on my head!" It was fun and exciting.

We even tried to one up each other when it came to stocking up on sex toys. We went to Home Depot and were going up and down the aisles trying to freak the other out. We got 100 feet of this thick, heavy rope to tie each other up. We got duct tape. He bought these rubber gloves that go up to the elbow as a joke and I was like, "What are you going to do with those?!" We bought phone wire and I was like, "OK, I come home and you will be hiding in the closet with a ski mask on and you'll come out and get me and tie me up with phone wire!"

When we got home and got at it we were making so much noise. I was screaming, the headboard was banging on the wall, and the furniture was getting thrown all over the place. I'm normally really quiet. I never had guys over. No one in my building knew what I did for a living. I kept it very safe and quiet at my place. But when Evan got there, all that went out the window. We were so loud that the neighbors started complaining and my landlord Dave—he reminded us of Mr. Roper from *Three's Company*—came to my door.

"There's a lot of noise in here, and that's unusual," Dave said.

Evan walked out naked with a towel on his dick and goes, "Is it?"

Dave didn't know what to think. He left but he must have come back a dozen more times over the four days we spent holed up in my apartment having sex. On day two, he said he heard me screaming and thought Evan was killing me. In fact, I like to get choked during sex, so he was hearing screaming and gasping for air, but it was all good. Dave knocked on our door for the zillionth time and said to Evan, "Are you hurting her?" Evan was so fed up with all the interruptions by then that he cracked back to Dave, "Maybe I am, but she likes it!"

And that's when the cops got called for the first time.

Two cops showed up: a jarhead-looking Robocop and a Mexican cop who actually seemed kind of cool. They said that several neighbors reported what they thought might be a domestic dispute. Evan pulled the Mexican cop aside and said, "Hey, here's the deal. We've been talking on the phone for three months and this is our first time together." He loved telling our story to anyone. And he goes, "Have you heard of Tera Patrick?" The cop got all wide-eyed and said, "Yes!" And Evan said, "Well, that's her in there." I came out and said hi and assured them that we were fine and they left.

It was the most incredible time. It was very emotional, too. I cried. I felt things I had never felt before. And I knew that he was going to marry me. I know this sounds crazy, but I prayed for Evan. I really did. I would lie in bed awake at night and cry and think, "What man is going to want to marry me? A porn star? The biggest porn star in the business? Who is going to take me home to their mother? "Hi, Mom. This is Linda, uh, Tera, uh, the star of *Sex Island*. But she's really nice, Mom, really." It scared me. It terrified me, actually. I wondered who was going to love me for me.

At the end of Evan's first stay with me, I remember lying down side-by-side with him, just holding each other. I looked up at him and he looked down at me, and he said, "You know when you're the most beautiful? When you're not trying to be."

EVAN SEINFELD

I arrived at Long Beach Airport, just thirty miles south of Los Angeles, and I was waiting for Tera. I saw this smoking hot chick in a silver 360 Modena Ferrari go zipping past. And I got excited. The phone rings and it's Tera. I pick up and ask her, "Was that you in the silver Ferrari?"

She told me, "No, I'm in an Infiniti QX4."

I thought, "Damn. I wanted to drive that Ferrari." And I started feeling anxious all over again. She could still be a cow. But my anxiety only lasted a minute. The Infiniti appeared, pulled up to the curb, and I looked at her through the windshield and my heart melted. Jenna Jameson didn't know what the fuck she was talking about. And I was a fool for even worrying about it.

In my fantasies, if I were to draw up the perfect woman, I couldn't even have imagined a woman as perfect as Tera. She had the exotic look I loved. Her skin was gorgeous. Her hair was so beautiful and soft. Even sitting down in the driver's seat, I could tell she was tall and statuesque, but still petite and tight on her frame. Supermodels want to look like this girl. I saw my wildest dreams incarnated in Tera Patrick. She had it all—a beautiful mind, body, and soul.

I got in the car and I was just mesmerized by her. She looked like a movie star. It felt like heaven. It took me to a place I've never been. I just sat across from her and took it all in. It was sensory overload. I smelled her. She didn't smell like perfume. She didn't have that bad perfume smell that all the girls before her had. She just smelled gorgeous. She smelled like some shampoo that's so expensive I'd never heard of it, clean and natural and incredibly sexy. I was completely erect just from smelling her. It was really love at first sniff.

And I couldn't keep my hands to myself. We were groping and touching and kissing as she drove. We'd been talking for three months on the phone. I was done talking. I was ready to start the humping. She was nervous, and it turned me on that she was nervous. But I couldn't help but think, "What's wrong with her? No chick could be this good looking and available. Maybe she has Tourette's syndrome or terrible gas. Maybe she has a tail. Maybe her pussy looked like a bulldog eating porridge." I didn't even know what that meant, but I feared it. What did I do to have the most beautiful girl in the world interested in me and turned on by me? I was so in love with her already. It felt too good to be true.

When we opened the door I was struck at how "Americana" she had her place decorated. It was almost Martha Stewart–esque. She had all of these vintage American items from the '50s like old Hershey's chocolate syrup signs on the wall. I didn't care. It was her, and all I wanted to do was rip her clothes off. I tore them off her like a savage animal. We started fucking all over the house. We broke furniture. We broke mirrors. It looked like a crime scene. We were going at each other, back and forth. Tera was very aggressive with me and she wanted me to be aggressive with her. She wanted me to fuck her as hard as I could and not stop. We broke the headboard off the bed. I threw my back out and I didn't want to tell her. I didn't want her to think of me as "Old Man Seinfeld" with his Jewish ailments. It was crazy.

I'm the overaggressive "sex addict" to start with and I'd never felt intimidated by a girl—ever. But here I am with this girl who fucked professional fuckers, so I felt like I had to outfuck the pros. I was like, "Yeah? You like that shit? Who's your daddy?" We had sex for four days and nights. I had spent my whole sexual life trying to recapture the feeling I had when I was thirteen and lost my virginity. And with Tera, I'd finally done it; only it was so much better this time.

Tera and I went at it so loud and long that the cops came. That's how you know you're having great sex: when the cops come. She was screaming. I was grunting and groaning. Her landlord Dave was a bully. He just kept knocking on our door complaining about the noise. We must have had twenty-five interruptions in those four days between Dave and the cops. Dave would find any reason to bother us. One time he complained that the car was parked an inch over the line, but mostly he kept coming back because it sounded like I was killing Tera inside.

When the cops showed up the first time, I explained our story to them and how this was our first time having sex after just talking on the phone for months. Tera came out in her robe, smiles at the cops, and said, "Hiiiiii!" I looked at one cop and go, "You get it now?" He looked at his partner and said, "There's nothing to see here."

Tera and I went back at it. We did everything. We were being silly, taking these photos of each other. We were having a lot of fun. I was trying to take a P.O.V. picture of myself peeing on her. Some people don't understand what peeing is all about. Peeing on each other isn't about the pee. It's about domination and submission. It's when she lays down on the floor of the shower and gives herself fully and says, "Go ahead do whatever you want. I'm yours." We are a perfect match because I am so overdominant and she is super-submissive All of her friends' worst fears came true: I made her my cock puppet. But she loved it.

It was so different for me. We were so connected. It was different from anything I'd ever done and I've fucked hundreds of girls. I was never a fan of the missionary position, but Tera loves it and I grew to love it. I think I wasn't a fan before because I didn't care about the girls I fucked so I didn't want to look them in the face. But I love missionary with Tera because I love looking at her. It was really emotional. We were falling deeper in love.

I was a little confused, though. I didn't know what to call her. I had been calling her Linda on the phone, but I also called her Tera. I met her as Tera, but now here I was someone special to her so I thought that maybe I should call her Linda and be the only one who does. I was confused. I kept going back and forth. I think she wanted me to call her Linda.

When she brought me to the airport at the end of our four days, I said to her, "I hope this doesn't sound crazy and I hope this isn't too soon and I hope I don't fuck this up, but I think I'm in love with you."

CHAPTER 15

Trust

TERA: The following weekend, I flew out to Brooklyn to visit Evan. He took me on a motorcycle ride around Manhattan on his gorgeous West Coast Chopper built by Jesse James. We pulled up to the club Lotus and ran into Dante Ross, who was Erik's producer, though I didn't know it at the time. Evan introduced me to Dante as "my girlfriend, Tera." Dante looked me up and down and clearly recognized my name and who I was. He must have called Erik right away because the next thing I knew Erik started blowing up my phone and leaving dozens of messages—thirty to be exact. "You fucking whore. I know you're with another guy. What's going on? Call me back." I never called him back.

Evan had run out for an errand and I was alone in his loft in the Williamsburg area of Brooklyn, freaking out over Erik's barrage of messages. There was no way I was going to call him back or pick up the phone. Since Erik didn't respect me, I didn't give him the respect to tell him I had moved on. I didn't think I owed him anything. Erik had been on tour when I met Evan and he wasn't calling me that much, and I wasn't calling him. I never officially broke it off with him because I didn't want a confrontation. It was just easier to move on quietly and let what we had fizzle into oblivion.

———

EVAN: When I first met Tera, I didn't know she was dating Erik. She didn't tell me anything about her dating life. She kept it kind of vague. When I came back to the loft that day, she was clearly upset and had been crying. I asked her what was wrong and she said, "I don't want to tell you. You'll get mad." At that point in our relationship, there was nothing she could tell me that would get me mad. I was in love with this girl. She said, "Well, I was dating someone before you and he won't stop calling." OK, no big deal, I thought. "And um, you know him," she said. Oh, great. It's always sticky if your girl dated someone you know, but it's nothing you can't get over if you want to get over it.

"Just tell me, it's OK," I said calmly.

"It's Erik, er, Everlast," she said. I could tell she was scared to say his name.

TERA: I was scared. I was already in love with Evan and I was really afraid that Evan would break up with me. I thought this was the make-or-break moment for our relationship. He was either going to leave me and say, "Fuck you and all your drama" or he was going to man up and support me and say, "No worries. We can handle this together. I'll take care of it."

I wasn't playing one off the other, either. I honestly didn't think Erik would care if I was dating someone else. He never cared while we were together, why would he care now? I told Evan, "Listen, you are the one I want to be with. I've been over him for a while now. I don't want to be with him." And Evan trusted me.

This was the first time I turned to him to help me handle my shit. And when he did, I realized what a strong man I had in Evan. He made me feel safe, and I needed that.

―――――――

EVAN: I just thought, OK, well, I've known him for a decade. My band Biohazard and his band House of Pain toured together in 1994 and we were all friends. Erik and I weren't boys, though. He was just a little less friendly than his band mates, but I didn't have any animosity toward him. Even though this would be awkward, I knew what I had to do. I had to give him a call and straighten this out.

It was a Sunday afternoon and I called him up. Erik put on his hip-hop voice and said, "Who dis?"

"It's Evan."

He got quiet.

"Why you calling my house on a Sunday?"

"You know why. It just came to my attention you're blowing up my girl's phone. Thirty messages from you? She ain't seeing you no more, she's with me."

This was awkward for me, too. I'm not the kind of guy who wants to step on another guy's territory, but this wasn't that situation. I knew Tera was telling me the truth when she said they hadn't been seeing each other.

"This is my girl and I love her. Don't call her anymore," I told him.

I remember him saying something like, "I ain't sweating her. I don't give a fuck about her. She's just some porno bitch," he said, sounding like a hurt guy. He was so negative. Then he said, "Y'all two are mad corny."

"'Corny'? What do you mean 'corny'? What the hell?"

"Ya'll just corny, both of you. If I see y'all at the club, you all should bounce."

"Dude, I haven't seen you in a club in ten years. Just stop calling."

(That was the last she heard from Erik, until five years later in 2008 when Tera cohosted a party at Mandalay Bay in Las Vegas for a tattoo parlor opening and she had to introduce both Everlast and my new band the Spyderz. We never saw him, talked to him, or heard from his camp that night, though.)

TERA: As I said Everlast's name on the mike that night in 2008, all I could think about was, "You said no one would want to marry a porn star? Evan was man enough to." I felt good. I won out in the end.

While Evan and I didn't fight over Erik or my past, we did fight about his past. I had the green-eyed monster in me when I first met Evan. I think I was so insanely jealous because I was so afraid of losing this amazing man. I couldn't believe this fairy-tale romance was real. I was very skeptical of it and had a hard time accepting the love he was trying to give me.

Our very first fight happened shortly after we met, when I was visiting him in Brooklyn. He was on the phone with his ex-girlfriend and I overheard him say to her, "Listen, I'm in love. I'm with Tera now. You're gorgeous. You'll find someone else." Apparently, his ex-girlfriend wanted Evan back and Evan was turning her down gently. In my warped mind, instead of being happy at hearing him say he's happy now and not to call him, I latched on to the "you're gorgeous" part of that call and flipped out on him. I turned around and spat venom at Evan: "Who is gorgeous? Who are you talking to?"

"Uh, it's my ex. I'm telling her I'm with you," he said.

"Why are you talking to your ex in front of me?" I screamed. I completely overreacted and freaked out on him. "How dare you tell her she's gorgeous? You are never to talk to your ex again." I was irrational and I just went off.

He was like, "OK, you're right. I'll never speak to her again."

Looking back on it now, I can't believe how crazy jealous and insecure I would get on him and how he always handled it the same way: with compassion, understanding, and respect. Evan had the patience of a saint with me. Any other man would've left my insecure bullshit and me. But Evan called me on that bullshit and gave me what I needed in a relationship: love, support, and, at the time, constant reassurance. He handled me like a pro. He always made me feel better and made me trust him and he never did cheat on me or do anything wrong. But it took a while before I could believe it was true. It took me a while to really trust that I found the one thing I was searching for my whole life: a man to treat me well and whom I could love until death do us part.

CHAPTER 16

The Happiest Girl in the World

I really did know that Evan would be my husband on that first night together. I never believed in that until it happened to me. With Evan, I just knew it. My previous two engagements to Clayton and Roland didn't even count. I was young and naïve then, and even though I accepted their proposals, deep down I never felt that either of them was the one. Besides, there was always a side of me that wanted to wait until I was older to get married because I had seen what getting married too young did to my parents.

Evan and I were inseparable during the first few months of our relationship. It was a passionate, crazy, emotional, sex-crazed time. I wanted to spend more time with Evan and less time working, but Digital Playground was making it hard for me. I'd be preparing to fly to New York to see Evan, and my manager, Sam, would all of a sudden have a job for me that weekend. It felt like she was trying to keep us apart. But there were certain jobs I just had to do, such as appearing at the Venus adult film expo in Berlin, Germany, in October 2002. I was booked in Germany for two full weeks, and I didn't want to be apart from Evan for that long, but Sam made me go.

I was busy every day at Venus signing autographs, meeting distributors, and schmoozing. And I was calling Evan constantly. I missed him so much and I was going through my jealousy phase, which was making me insecure about being apart. Instead of going to any of the Venus parties or events, I would stay in my hotel room, talking to Evan for hours. We were still in the honeymoon period of our relationship, as it had only been a month since our first date and we were head-over-heels in love.

Evan called me constantly too. We both just missed each other a lot and loved to hear the sound of the other's voice. One day on this trip, I called Evan and he wasn't there. No worries. He usually calls back immediately. I figured maybe he was just in the bathroom or the shower or something. But then an hour went by and still no Evan. Two hours went by and I began to think the worst: He's with another girl! I was getting furious, and each message to him got more frantic. I started out all sweet and loving, "Hi, Evan, it's me. I miss you. Call me." And by the time I left my fifth message it was, "Where the fuck are you? What the fuck are you doing? You better not be with another girl! You fucking asshole!"

Twenty-four hours later, I called his cell again and his friend Robey picked up. I said, "Where the fuck is Evan? What the fuck is going on?" He told me Evan was in the hospital. Evan and his friend Tyson Beckford, the model, were taking the air conditioner out of his Brooklyn loft because I had complained it was too drafty in there and Tyson dropped it on Evan's foot and broke his toe.

I felt like a fool. Here's this man doing something sweet for me to make my visits to Brooklyn more comfortable, and I'm thinking he's out gallivanting with some chick. I felt horrible and told myself that I had to stop being so crazy and just trust this man. That made me miss Evan even more.

I missed him so much that I slept with my phone so I wouldn't miss his call. But one morning I woke up and my phone wasn't in my bed. I panicked. Sam told me that I must have dropped my phone somewhere and not to worry; we'd report it stolen and get a new one.

Later that day, Sam left her purse in the back of the cab and a phone fell out (but we didn't know it at the time). Next thing I know, I'm borrowing Sam's phone to call Evan and before I can dial, the phone rings. I wouldn't normally answer someone else's phone but it was in my hand, so I picked up. I didn't notice that when the call came in, it said TERA CELL on the screen, but it must have because it was the cab company calling to say they found a phone and dialed the last number called to try to find the owner. I asked what number it was, and they read me *my* number. I was shocked. Sam had apparently taken my phone and hid it in her purse. I told them I'd be right there to pick it up and then I called Evan and said, "I want to come home right now."

I had my suspicions about Digital and Sam, but that incident made it clear to me that it was time to leave. I called her out on the phone situation and she admitted that she had taken it. She said, "Well, I saw how much you were talking to Evan and I thought it was really unhealthy, so I was just trying to protect you." She had a great way of manipulating me. I told Sam, "You need to let me live my life. I really love this guy. He's not a bad guy. He's really good to me. Why can't you be happy for me?"

I was furious and couldn't wait to get home. But when I called Evan, he had something else in mind. "Don't go home to California. Come to Miami with me," he said. "I want to take you on a nice vacation. You need to get away."

He met me at the airport on crutches from his broken toe. My heart melted at the sight of him. I didn't care where we were going or what we were going to do. All I wanted was to be together. But he had more in store. He went all out and booked a king suite with an ocean view at one of Miami Beach's most upscale and elite resorts: the Art Deco Delano Hotel. It was one of the most beautiful hotels I had ever seen. It looked like a scene from an Old Hollywood movie starring some blond starlet like Veronica Lake in a white silk robe, walking around in marabou and satin slippers with a kitten heel, and smoking out of one of those fancy long cigarette holders. The suite was elegant in all white with sheer curtains that hung from ceiling to floor and a huge king bed with big fluffy white down covers and inviting pillows. Even the floor tiles were white. It was so pristine that I didn't want to touch anything. It was simply stunning. And Evan had the room set up with all of my favorites—fresh strawberries, champagne, and rose petals. I was floored.

Of course, we couldn't wait to tear each other's clothes off, so we had sex immediately. In the middle of our romp, there was a knock on the door. I ignored it, but Evan stopped fucking me and jumped up. Evan usually doesn't stop for anything. The house could be burning down and he'd keep on going.

"Don't you get that," I said.

"I have to!" He seemed anxious and started to head for the door. I didn't want him to leave so I grabbed his arm and pulled him toward me. I'm a lot stronger than you'd think. He broke free so I lunged for his leg. As he made his way toward the door, there I was clinging comically to his leg and stopping him from getting very far. There's another knock on the door. Evan finally broke free and with nothing on but a towel covering his still-erect penis, he opens the door to find a bellboy with a FedEx package. He ripped open the envelope, and I could see there was a ring box inside. Before he could say anything, I knew what was about to happen. I knew this was the moment in my life that I would never forget. I was about to become the happiest girl in the world.

He took the ring out, got down on one knee, slipped the ring on my finger, and said, "Linda, will you marry me?"

"Yes! Of course!" I said. I had been waiting for this moment my whole life. It was the perfect proposal: simple and surprising. I couldn't believe it was happening to me. I had spent so many years crying myself to sleep, praying for a man like Evan to spend my life with, and here was the moment. I couldn't have been any happier. We went out to dinner that night to celebrate with friends.

The next day, we drove to Evan's parents' house in Boynton Beach, Florida. It was so nice to be with a man who was proud to introduce me to his family. They were completely blown away that we got engaged so fast. It had only been two months since we met in person for the first time and five months since we started our phone courtship. They were supportive, but understandably surprised. We started talking about wedding plans immediately. Knowing neither of us had a lot of money at the time, Evan's mother, Lois, said, "Oh, I have a great idea. To save money, you can wear Elena's wedding dress."

She did not just say that! Elena? Really? Elena?!

Elena was Evan's ex-wife and mother of his son, Sammy. My eyes welled up when Lois said that, and poor Evan was beyond mortified. ("She was just being a cheap Jew," Evan said to me about it later.) Later in the evening, Lois whispered to Evan, "I'm not going to get attached." I didn't take it personally. Evan didn't exactly have a good track record with women. His dad, Ira, used to call the constant turnover of girls in his life "The Girlfriend of the Month Club." But I was different. I was here to stay, and I knew he wasn't going anywhere. His mother would eventually learn this too. It was just a matter of time.

(Evan had already met my dad, under inauspicious circumstances. Shortly after we met, Evan was visiting me at my condo in Sherman Oaks. We had just finished having sex . . . that's all we did back then, have sex and order food from Pink Dot, a famous delivery service in the L.A. area that delivers you anything, anytime, in this weird little blue-and-pink polka-dot car.

Evan heard a key enter the lock at my front door. He bolted out of bed, stark naked, and asked me, "Where's your bat?"

"Bat? What bat?"

In Brooklyn, Evan kept a bat by his bed. I didn't have one, so he grabbed the most lethal-looking item he could find in my apartment: a large, heavy stone ashtray.

"Who's there?" he asked.

"It's David. I'm coming in," a man said.

"I don't know no David," Evan snapped.

"I have the keys. I'm coming in," he replied.

As the door started to open, Evan held the ashtray cocked overhead in one hand and swung open the door with the other, which made the man literally fall into the condo. He grabbed the long-haired, hippie-looking man by the neck and hung him over the balcony railing and said, "You better start talking."

By this time I'd emerged from the bedroom to find Evan holding my father over the railing.

Evan turned beet red. He immediately let go of him, apologized profusely, and we all had a good laugh about it. My dad had come to the condo that night to get his car keys because he'd left his car in my garage when he went on a trip to Hawaii. He didn't want to wake us by calling, so he used the set of keys I had given him. Not exactly the best way for Evan to meet the father of his future bride.)

I was the happiest I'd been in a long time, but at the same time I felt really sad that I didn't have anyone to share my news with and those I did tell were skeptical because we were moving so fast. I'd call up "friends" with the big news, and the reaction would typically go like this: "Come again? You're engaged? Tera, you just met this guy. That is crazy."

It might have seemed crazy, but sometimes crazy pans out. Why is it so hard to believe that you can meet someone and fall in love instantly? When you know, you know.

Nobody believed in us in the beginning, but that only made our bond even stronger. It felt like Evan and me against the world, and I liked that. What people don't realize about Evan is that he may come off tough and in charge, but if it weren't for him, I wouldn't have found my true independence and strength. He helped empower me to take control of my life and of my career and helped me become a better woman in the process. He got me through the toughest times in my life. He wasn't the one marrying me because I was a porn star. I was the one marrying him because he was a rock star, and I always wanted to marry a rock star. I just got lucky that my rock star was also my rock in life. The one solid thing I could always count on for all of my needs.

CHAPTER 17

The Storm Before the Calm

In November of 2002, I called my manager, Sam, and told her that I was no longer going to be with Digital Playground. I liked the break I had taken, and now I was in love and getting married and I thought this was my chance at having a normal life. I didn't want to work for Digital anymore. I didn't want to be in the porn industry. I just wanted to be in love and play house with my new man. Of course, I was under contract so it wasn't going to be that easy to get away. She told me I was making a big mistake and not to trust Evan, that he was a rock star who would just cheat on me.

Despite what had happened in Germany, I was actually surprised at Sam's reaction when I told her I wanted out. Digital Playground wasn't just my manager and production company, it had been like my family, especially Sam. I honestly thought she'd be happy for me that I met a great guy and fell in love and that she would want for me what I wanted for myself. That is what a friend does. That is what your closest confidante does. That is what your "mother figure" does. That is what I expected Sam to do. I expected her to support me. But instead she supported Digital.

Leaving Digital also meant leaving my cohosting gig on Playboy

TV's *Night Calls,* which I loved. My last episode taped the last week of December. My contract had expired, and *Playboy* didn't renew it because I wasn't with Digital anymore. But it was OK. I was ready to move on and make a clean break.

Evan said to me, "Look, I don't want to get into your business, but you need help. Where I come from, your manager and your production company shouldn't be the same thing. You have a conflict of interest here. And I don't think they are going to let you go that easily." He was right, and things got nasty pretty quickly.

I just cried. "My life is over, isn't it?"

"It's not over, but it's going to cost you a lot of money to defend this and we don't have the money," he said.

I can't go into the legalities of it, but I was able to keep some money that I had in the bank. I got rid of my condo in Sherman Oaks, got rid of the Infiniti that Digital leased for me, and moved in with Evan in Brooklyn for the next year or so.

Digital filed a breach of contract lawsuit against me that same month, and we countersued for damages. I was ready to just give up. I didn't think I had a chance and was just too tired to fight.

But then Evan sat me down and said, "Listen, I love you very much and I just want you to realize that no matter where you go in the world, no matter what you do, you're always going to be Tera Patrick. Don't give up on that. We will fight this together. You should really think about capitalizing on who you are. Everybody else has made money from you, and I know you want to give up and never want to work again and I know you're really enjoying your life right now, but you should really go out and fight for what is rightfully yours."

Even though I had been on a self-imposed hiatus leading up to this mess, I still knew that I would want to reenter the business at some point. The big deal for me, and what made me fight so hard, was that they wanted to take my name. I created the name and worked very hard to get to this point in my career. I couldn't stand the thought of them owning my name and being allowed to make money off of me for the rest of my life. The thought of that drove me crazy.

I'll admit it, once the fog lifted and I looked at my situation, I got pissed as hell for being so naïve as to have signed such a bad deal. I was so angry with myself. And I was so resentful at my situation. That's why I tried to hurt myself. I felt so stupid. Why wasn't I smarter? I went from not having the fight in me to fighting mad to suicidal in a matter of months. I knew I was on a slippery slope, so I decided to stop drinking and smoking pot. I quit cold turkey. I had to fight this with a clear head and sound mind. But I couldn't do it alone.

Alcoholics Anonymous helped me with that. It didn't get off to a great start when I went to my first AA meeting in Brooklyn in January 2003 completely high as a kite. I was very nervous about attending this meeting so I smoked a joint before I went. It sounded like a good idea at the time, and I'm sure I wasn't the first person to get high before a meeting. Evan didn't notice at first. I kept it cool for the drive over. But as we settled into the metal folding chairs at the meeting and my high kicked in further, Evan caught me staring at the plate of doughnuts on the table for an inappropriate amount of time.

"Oh my God. Are you high?" he whispered in my ear.

"I'm totally wasted!" I laughed. I thought it was funny. It wasn't.

He just had this look on his face like, "OK. I'm sorry, but the answer we're looking for is *not* wasted."

I couldn't understand a single thing the speaker said. As the gentleman told his story about being addicted to meth, my thoughts shifted from "I wonder if there's any coffee left?" to "Those doughnuts are probably stale but stale doughnuts are better than no doughnuts" to "My butt hurts from sitting on this chair" to "My mouth is so dry, where is the water?" to "Meth? Shit, that's fucked up. At least I'm not on meth!"

At the end of the meeting, a guy came up to me and said, "Tera, I'm your biggest fan. Will you sign my AA book?" So much for the "anonymous" part of AA. I was creeped out and vowed to never go to a coed AA meeting ever again. My paranoid mind thought my fans were everywhere, and maybe they were. But Evan encouraged me to try a different meeting and give AA a second chance. "Maybe you'll find fellowship at a different meeting," he said. "Fellowship" is "friendship" in AA terms.

So the next meeting I tried was a women-only meeting on Park Avenue. I figured those "ladies who lunch" in their Chanel suits, conservative pumps, and fur coats don't watch porn, and my identity would be safe there. I was right.

I'd never been to Park Avenue before, but when I walked into the meeting and saw such a diverse mix of women all chatting amicably in low, soothing voices, it felt nice. It felt serene. It felt safe. There were no creepy guys there to recognize me. I doubted these ladies had watched a minute of porn in their lives. I sat down next to a distinguished-looking woman with white hair, salmon-colored slacks, and a very proper blouse. It felt so Park Avenue to me, and that was a good thing. The woman immediately embraced me and said, "Hello, dear. Welcome to the Park Avenue meeting. You're a new face. Tell us about yourself."

Oh, great. It was nice to be welcomed, but the worst part about being new to a meeting is that you're encouraged to "share," and I wasn't exactly comfortable sharing my story. I had to say *something*, so I started with the expected: "Hi. I'm Linda. I'm an alcoholic and addicted to marijuana."

"Hi, Linda," the group said in unison.

I was just going to give the basics: "I live in Brooklyn with my fiancé and my stepson. I just moved here from L.A. and I don't really know anyone. I'm just trying to get through the days." There, I "shared." But then something came over me. I somehow found myself pouring my heart out and sharing my whole story. These women seemed so warm and understanding to me. And I especially felt a lot of support and comfort from the white-haired woman next to me. It's hard to describe, but I could feel her giving me strength. She was very attentive, and I could tell she was sincere. We connected. I continued on to tell the group about everything—my lawsuit, my craziness, my relationship, everything. I started out telling them a little white lie that I was a model, but by the time I was done sharing they knew all about my porn career. I feared their judgment, but they couldn't care less. No one judged me. This was a group of women where one was a sex addict, another had a twenty-year battle with booze and drugs, another woman was sleeping with her husband's friends, and so on and so on. Everyone had their own issues and demons, and mine didn't seem so big after all.

After I told my story, everyone clapped. I felt oddly at home. The woman in salmon next to me officially introduced herself to me. "Hi, Linda. I'm 'Sandy.' So, you do porn? Well, that woman over there is married to a famous musician. And the girl over there used to be a singer. . . ." And "Sandy" (as I'll call her) proceeded to tell me who's who and then she said, "You didn't think you were the only one into sex, drugs, and rock-and-roll, now did you?" I felt relieved, and we exchanged numbers.

Sandy became a real anchor for me while I was in Brooklyn. I went to the Park Avenue meeting regularly and talked to her all the time. I liked AA, and I found peace there. And I found a new friend, one who was older and wiser. She was more experienced, had a broader outlook on the world, and put things in perspective. She was like a mother to me.

That year for my birthday I chose to celebrate it with an intimate dinner with just Evan and Sandy and her husband, who both showed up in matching salmon outfits. I still talk to Sandy occasionally to this day.

Evan was right. I found fellowship in AA. It guided me through a difficult time and helped me stop abusing alcohol and pot. I didn't drink or get high for two years. But that didn't mean I didn't have *other* demons to deal with.

One cold February day at Evan's loft in Brooklyn in 2003, we got a call from my attorney, and the details of the case just overwhelmed me. I lost it. I remember thinking that they had won and my life was over. I decided to end my life and end the misery I had been in. It felt easier to quit than to fight. I was so angry that I just wanted to hurt myself. All of these intense emotions came over me and I went into a rage. I don't remember what happened next. But Evan will never forget, so I'll let him tell the rest of this story. . . .

EVAN SEINFELD

Before I can explain what happened next, let me back up a bit. Leading up to her mental breakdown and suicide attempt, she was all over the map emotionally. On her good days, she was really excited to be in love and she was happy nesting in my Brooklyn loft. She kept herself busy by decorating, cleaning, shopping, and cooking for Sammy and me. When she was feeling "up," we'd go out to parties and dinners or stay in and have sex all night.

On her bad days, the legal drama with Digital Playground would get her down and she'd spend the entire day in bed or she'd cry uncontrollably and break down, asking, "Why is this happening to me? How could I have been so stupid?" And on her *really* bad days, her feelings would turn into crazy, irrational thoughts and violent outbursts. It was like a switch would turn on in her head and she'd have a detached, vacant look on her face like she was looking right through me. When she got that look, when that switch turned on, there was no reaching her. She would begin to say irrational things and start accusing me of being part of the problem. I was always defending myself. Tera's way when things got her down or when bad things happened was to lash out at those closest to her.

"You know what? You're just like everybody else!" she'd scream at me.

"I'm your fiancé. I love you. I'm trying to help you," I would try to explain.

"Yeah, well you probably just want to see what you can get out if it." She was relentless.

These episodes started getting more and more severe, and each one would last longer than the previous one. She'd turn that anger toward me and start screaming about how she hated me. She'd threaten to leave me, but then she'd snap out of it and have these moments of clarity and apologize. She was under extreme emotional stress, and I felt helpless.

When she got *really* worked up, she'd start throwing things at me. One day, she picked up a twelve-pound glass candle holder and clocked me in the head with it. It knocked me loopy.

"What the fuck is the matter with you?" I yelled. I don't think she knew why she did what she did at this time.

She continued her assault, throwing more candle holders, my bass guitar, mirrors, whatever she could get her hands on, including a blackjack—a piece of lead wrapped in leather that I kept in the apartment for protection. She grabbed the blackjack and threw it at me. But she missed and hit a piece of Plexiglas that shattered all over the apartment. When she saw that she missed, she came at me swinging and clawing.

"Fine! I'll just kill myself," she said as she lunged at me and pulled me with her as she hurled herself down the stairs in the loft. We fell head over heels and hit the ground *really* hard. She was out to hurt herself, and she was taking me down with her. After we recovered from the fall, her rage continued.

With tears rolling down her face, she threatened, "I'm going to call the cops!"

"But *you're* attacking *me!*" I tried to reason with her.

"They'll never believe that, because I'm the girl," she replied.

"And then they'll arrest me and you'll be all alone in this insanity. At least I'm here trying to help you!" I said as I tried to hold on to her so she would calm down.

"GET OFF ME!!!"

That was when I realized her problems were more than I was able to handle. I called our family therapist, Nelson Lugo, for some advice. Nelson is this wonderful Puerto Rican psychiatrist who I used when Sammy was having a hard time with my divorce from his mother. Nelson told me that I had to be careful Tera didn't hurt herself or others because there was no way to reason with a person suffering like this. I would call Nelson regularly during this time and talk to him about Tera's recurring episodes, and he said it sounded like she was having a nervous breakdown. I agreed.

When she did come out of these episodes and have a moment of clarity, she'd feel horrible and be hyper-apologetic. She'd apologize and say, "I'm sorry! I don't know why I did that." She'd write me little "I'm sorry" cards and dote on me for a while. She didn't know what she was doing. Some nights she would go to bed mad as hell at me and then wake up all lovey-dovey, make me breakfast, and give me another huge apology note or flowers. I have tons of her apology notes. They'd often say "I'm sorry. I don't know why you stay with me. I'm a crazy bitch. I'm going through a lot of shit right now. I don't know what's happening with me."

When Biohazard was on tour in the UK in the fall of 2002, Tera came out on the road with me. One night in a London hotel, we were having sex and everything was great, and then that switch went off and she started getting angry with me and physically attacking me. She was really jealous at the time so I think the fight was out of some sort of jealous rage. She scratched me so hard that she drew blood on my face and my chest. She flung herself on me and was scratching and clawing at me. I never laid a hand on her. I just tried to calm her down, but her screams alerted hotel security and they called the police. The cops came and found Tera and me naked and scratched up. It looked bad. Then something clicked in her and she snapped out of it. She told the police, "Everything is OK. We were just having rough sex." The cops looked at me and saw the blood and scratches and asked, "Sir, do you want us to take *her* away?" Of course I told them no, and after that Tera apologized.

The last three weeks before her big incident, from the time we were in London until the meltdown that landed her in the hospital, I was like Edward Norton in *Fight Club*. I always had a new scar, bruise, or black eye.

All of this was just the precursor to the meltdown of all meltdowns—the day she finally snapped and had to be institutionalized. This is where Tera's a little fuzzy on the details. But here is how I remember it going down that night in the loft. Something set Tera off again. Maybe it was the phone call with the attorney like she remembers. But what she doesn't remember is that she took that anger and frustration out on me again and started swinging at me and scratching me. We were at the top of the stairs and she's attacking me and I'm trying to hold her back and we ended up falling down the stairs together . . . again. But this trip down the stairs was more serious. She was trying to kill herself. I just thought it was another freak-out, but it was way worse than that.

After our fall, she started throwing anything she could get her hands on. I was eventually able to get both of her hands behind her back and there was some duct tape lying around nearby (we used duct tape to tie each other up sometimes when we had sex, and duct tape is like the Swiss Army knife for musicians; we use it for everything). So I wrapped duct tape around her hands and threw her in the backseat of the Suburban and took her to St. Vincent's Hospital in Manhattan.

We got to the emergency room at the hospital, and Tera was still kicking and screaming. "I'm not the crazy one! It's him. He's the crazy one. Look, he tied me up," she told the nurses and cops. There are always cops in emergency rooms, and this night was no exception. When they saw Tera's hysterical state, the cops naturally looked at me as the bad guy and sat me down in a chair to question me.

"Guys, just go talk to her for five minutes and you'll understand completely who the crazy one is here," I told them.

They didn't know who to believe. To them, it must have looked like a scene from *Natural Born Killers*, like Mickey and Mallory, you know? Here's this big, bald, tattooed guy with scratches on his face, bleeding, with the prettiest Asian girl they've ever seen, duct taped to herself, screaming bloody murder.

So one of the cops pulled me aside and said, "What are you doing? You can't duct tape someone against their will. It's against the law. You should have called 911."

"It was a judgment call. I thought taking her to the hospital myself would be faster," I said. "Take the fucking tape off her and see what she does. Go ahead."

When things finally settled down, I had a chance to explain to them the emotional stress she had been under over her legal battles with Digital and how there had been many episodes leading up to this. I told them that I loved her very much and I would be there for her, but that she needed some serious help and she was a danger to herself. Tera would later admit that she was suicidal that night.

She ended up signing herself into the hospital, and they put her in the psychiatric ward for observation. She finally calmed down and fell asleep in her hospital bed and told me to go home. There was nothing else I could do. She spent two weeks in the psych ward at St. Vincent's, and things got better after that.

CHAPTER 18

What Have I Done?

Once the mayhem of being admitted to the psych ward at St. Vincent's subsided and I realized I did need help, my doctors sat me down and told me that I was suffering a series of symptoms similar to bipolar disorder, though I've never officially been diagnosed as bipolar, then or now. When they explained the symptoms to me, I knew instantly it's what I've been suffering from all along. It explained my crazy highs and lows, my wild spending, the way I would act out sexually, and my depression. I remember the doctor asking me a series of questions and one by one I answered yes to them all with a growing pit in the bottom of my stomach. He asked: Do you have sex a lot? Do you shop a lot? Do you overreact? Are you easily agitated? Do you throw things? Can you not control yourself at times? Yes, yes, yes, yes, yes, and yes. It clicked, and I cried about it a lot. I couldn't believe that I was so psychologically damaged.

I thought a lot about my mom during my two weeks in the hospital because my mom has all of these symptoms too. I guess it was just in my genes. They say there are five stages of grief, and that is exactly what I went through when I processed this diagnosis. The first stage is denial. I certainly thought the problem was everyone else, not me. I didn't think I was wrong in my outbursts against Evan. I didn't think I was acting crazy.

The second stage is anger. Evan can, and has, attested to that one. I was angry at Digital Playground, angry at myself, angry at the world, and then angry at the one person who loved me enough to stand by me, help me, and believe in me.

The next stage is bargaining. I begged to get out of the hospital and promised I'd be better if they'd only let me out of there. The bargaining part was my "if only" phase. I'd tell my doctor: "If only I wasn't in this lawsuit, life would be so much better. If only I could work again, I'd have more money and that would make me happy. If only I wasn't on meds, I would have my appetite back. If only I could have my stepson full-time, it would make Evan happy and we'd be a happy family." I'd tell Dr. Nelson Lugo, "If you get me out of the hospital, I promise to be better." And then my overwhelming emotions would kick in and I'd flip on him and say, "If you don't get me out of this hospital now, I promise I'll kill you!" My bargaining turned to threats, and that kept me in the psych ward even longer.

The fourth stage is depression. Once it hit me how serious my situation had become, I went back to crying and curling up in a ball on my hospital bed. I spent several days in the hospital in the woe-is-me phase, feeling even more depressed than ever.

And of course, the final stage is acceptance. I finally came to accept my situation. I started taking the medicine they gave me, and it really did help.

Once I started following doctors' orders, my psychiatrist promised the hospital that he would look after me and suggested that I was stable enough to leave. Dr. Lugo said to me, "You know, Linda, you just have to accept that you have to face it and go on with your life." And I did. But not without one more outburst.

When I got home from St. Vincent's, I spit venom at Evan. "I can't believe you locked me up in that place! I hate you!"

"Oh, God. Here we go," he said.

Just when I thought I was understanding what was happening to me and feeling positive about it, along came those paranoid and angry feelings again. I don't think you can get better overnight or even in two weeks. And I do know that it takes a little bit of time for medicine to kick in and really begin to work. I think when I came home fighting mad, it was because I was still processing my situation and working through it.

Evan and I fought for days following my return from the hospital. We'd go round and round like this:

"You had me committed!"

"You needed to be committed! You were crazy!"

"Stop calling me crazy!"

"But you are. You needed help!"

"No, I didn't."

"If you don't get it together, I'm going to leave you because you're so crazy. I can't handle this anymore."

Deep down I knew he loved me so much, and I think I was afraid of that love. I was afraid to surrender myself to that love. We were fighting so bad that I made him sleep on the couch. I just couldn't deal, and I was so angry. It was the first time we didn't sleep together.

On our third day of fighting, I was looking down at him sleeping on the couch and he looked so exhausted. I had a moment of clarity. I felt like the worst person ever. I *am* crazy. Oh my God. I do need help. What have I done? This man loves me and was just trying to help me. I went to down to where he was sleeping and I kneeled beside him and woke him up. "You're right. I need help. Please help me and please don't leave me."

"I'm not going to leave you," he said. "I'm going to get you through this."

I knew I was in good hands: the hands of a strong man who loved me and who would help me get better. Evan made sure I took my medicine. He made sure I saw the therapist. He kept me positive. Evan vowed to help me get better and to become successful on my own terms. And that's exactly what we did.

2003 Diary Entries:

These are the diaries I kept in 2003 as I struggled with my craziness, adjusted to medication, and dealt with the lawsuit and my insecurities about Evan. The number of days noted in each entry was the number of days I'd been sober at the time of writing it.

April 19, 2003
105 days
I woke up crying. I'm not feeling good. I love Evan so much and I don't want to hurt him. I don't know why my emotions take such charge of me sometimes. I can't believe he feels this way about me. And I can't believe I disrespected him because I love him so much. I never want to hurt him. Maybe God will help me every day as long as I pay attention every day and help myself to keep my inner peace.
Love,
Linda

May 20, 2003
136 days
Woke up feeling good. Evan was obsessing about the car stereo. Well, he loves cars. Chopper [a black and white toy fox terrier that Evan gave me on Valentine's Day 2003] is going to school for three weeks. My little man needs it. Today is doctor day. I'm hoping to get some health insurance. I have a photo shoot tomorrow with Anneli. Glad to start my stuff and work again. I'm smiling a lot today. See? This is how I need to feel. Lots of love to you God.
I love you,
Linda

MAY 21, 2003

137 DAYS

Photo shoot day. Took my new medication and it made me not feel so good. I had to take a nap. Then I had a huge fight with Evan. I really realize how much he loves me and how much I love and need him. I love Evan so much and want to spend the rest of my life with him. I love you God. I'm going to write more later.

MAY 22, 2003

138 DAYS

Meeting with Jim Kohls and Mark Hamilton, 1:30 pm. President and VP of Hustler Media.

Had a pretty good meeting. Went to the party for Hustler and had a good time. Evan blew me away and tattooed my name Linda on his wrist. We left for New York. I love you God. Thank you for another great day.

MAY 23, 2003

139 DAYS

I just flew in from New York. We picked up Sam. I'm feeling pretty good. We're just going to have a mellow day. Evan is such a good dad. I love him so much. I hope I can be a good step mom. I can't stop thinking about pot. Oh my God. I hope it passes. I love you.

Love,

Linda

JUNE 1, 2003

148 DAYS

I slept in late today. We're going to write my press release. I felt OK. I'm having some episodes of moodiness. Thank you so much for everything God. I'm trying not to think about my case. It's so hard. This is the start of a new month. Summertime. Yay!

I love you,

Linda

JUNE 2, 2003

149 DAYS

I had a horrible night. Evan and I started major fighting. I went totally crazy. I don't know why I just can't be normal. I did not take my medication. I did not want to sleep at all. I love Evan. And I'm so angry with myself for hurting him. Please help me God.

Love,

Linda

JUNE 4, 2003

151 DAYS

I woke up so tired. I had to do VH1. I went to get my hair done and it turned out so beautiful. I'm so blond! I love it. I had a nice interview. I hope they cut it together nicely. I hate doing shows when they're not accurate. Evan did so well. I'm so proud of my baby and I love him so much. I went home and cleaned up and we had amazing sex. Thank you so much for everything.

Love,

Linda

JUNE 5, 2003

5 MONTHS. YAY!

I felt like I didn't get enough sleep. Looking forward, believe it or not, to a little travel. Digital Playground is trying to fight me again. Ugh. It never ends. Anyway, we picked up Sam and are having a fun day. Thank you God for everything.

Love you,

Linda

JUNE 7, 2003
154 DAYS

I had a nice day. I went to a new Pilates mat class, "Happy Now Flat Belly." I loved it. I miss my baby so much. Chopper and I are on our way to the airport to meet his trainer. Chopper goes to school for three weeks. I'm worried about court and I hope it all goes well. Thank you God for everything.

Love,
Linda

CHAPTER 19

Dancing Queen

After things started settling down after my return from St. Vincent's and my medicine started kicking in, I started feeling strong again. The fog was lifting and I was back in fighting-for-my-rights mode. Evan wasn't only my rock through all of this, but he also took over as my manager. Evan has managed his band Biohazard for years, so managing wasn't something new to him and I trusted him.

Evan had a very important thought one night. He said to me, "You're obviously a very powerful commodity. If you weren't so special and worth so much, these scumbags wouldn't be fighting so hard to keep you out of the business. So there's something here, and I really think we should get you back in business on your own terms." It was hard for me to see the light at the end of the tunnel at the time, but Evan knew what was at stake and that's why he fought so hard for me.

Evan started making phone calls and lining up allies. We needed people to be in the Tera Patrick camp if we were going to give my career another shot. Evan was calling on anyone and everyone he knew in the industry to get me work. One of his first calls was to his old friend Dan Davis, editor in chief of the adult magazine *Gen-*

esis. They made me masthead publisher and gave me a column, which I titled "Teravision." I was honored, and it was yet another way to express myself. It was a great chance to use my brains instead of just my body. It proved that I wasn't just some dumb porn chick, but that I could actually write and had something to say. I discovered a new talent that I never knew I had in me and felt proud that I could share my experiences in a positive light. And it paid well and we needed the cash. Over the next six years, I wrote approximately seventy columns, appeared on the cover a dozen times, and was featured in a bunch of layouts.

The next ally we found was my old friend Teri Weigel, the former *Playboy* Playmate and porn star who took me under her wing at my first AVN convention. She'd been in the industry for a while and I needed some sage advice on what to do next.

Teri asked me, "How are you making money right now?"

"I'm not," I said.

"You don't dance?" she asked.

"What do you mean?"

"What do you mean what do I mean? Are you doing feature dancing?" she asked.

Unlike many other porn stars, I didn't come from the world of strip clubs. In fact, I'd only been to a strip club with an ex-boyfriend a few times. It wasn't really my thing. I always thought that stripping was something you do in order to get into porn and not something you do once you're already a porn star like me.

"Feature dancing? What is that?" I asked.

"Oh, honey," said Teri. "When you're a huge star like yourself, you can make a ton of money doing feature dance shows. It's notches above stripping and you can make ten times the amount of money a regular stripper makes. You need to call this guy, Tony Lee. He's going to introduce you to a whole new world."

Tony Lee is the number-one booking agent for adult film stars on the feature dancing circuit. Evan had already spent all of the money he made from the last Biohazard tour, as well as his music publishing advance, on my legal bills, and we were running out of money. (We ended up spending about $300,000 to fight the suit.)

I soon found out that feature dancers are essentially special strippers. If you have a name and a following, the club makes a special event of your dancing engagement. You're paid a guaranteed fee. You get to keep 100 percent of the money on the stage and you do a meet-and-greet after your show where you sell the fans your merchandise: autographed photos, DVDs, posters, T-shirts, etc. And you get to keep all of that money too. It sounded like the perfect way to make some fast cash.

Evan called up Tony immediately. "Is Tony Lee there? This is Evan Seinfeld."

"This is Tony Lee. What can I do for you?" he answered.

"I'm Tera Patrick's manager, and Tera Patrick has expressed an interest in dancing," said Evan.

"Can you hold on for a second?" Tony said very businesslike. Tony must have just placed the phone down without hitting the hold button because the next thing Evan hears is this loud, "Whooooo hoooooo!" on the other end of the phone.

Tony got back on the phone, tried to play it cool, and said, "So, Tera Patrick is interested in dancing? This is the phone call I've been waiting for my entire career."

"There's one catch," Evan said.

"What's that?"

"We're in litigation with Digital Playground and—" Evan said.

Tony interrupted, "I know all about it and I don't care. I would love to work with you guys."

Tony Lee became my next ally, and he soon booked me on my first feature-dancing gig. He promised me that I would make more money than any other feature dancer ever did dancing and that I would be paying my legal bills and have money left over.

There was just one more problem. I didn't know how to dance.

Lisa Ann,
my stripper mentor

Tony wasn't concerned about that. He hooked me up with someone who could show me the ropes: Lisa Ann, a performer in the business who now runs a talent agency. Lisa Ann gave me a one-day crash course in what feature dancing is all about.

Our first stop was a sleazy lingerie store in Hollywood. She helped me pick pieces that were easy to get off and I ended up going with a four-piece outfit that consisted of a bra, panties, an overcoat/robe, a skirt, and, of course, five-inch stripper heels. I had one piece of clothing to take off for each of the four songs I would dance to. In the early days, I danced in themed costumes, such as a French maid, various schoolgirl outfits, and a few versions of a biker babe—one in leather and one in denim. My idea was to act out men's fantasies with these various personalities.

After we suited up, Lisa took me to the Spearmint Rhino strip club in Van Nuys to watch some of the girls there dance and hopefully pick up some tips. I took mental notes as the girls would twirl around the pole and do their splits on the shiny stage. I was inspired and excited at the idea of being the girl up there twirling around in fancy lingerie for a captive live audience. It was so different from performing for the camera.

I was intimidated by the strippers' more advanced moves, i.e., the upside-down pole work, splits, and other fancy footwork. I didn't know how I was going to pull off all that stripper trickery onstage. "Don't worry about it. You're a big star," Lisa Ann explained. "The fans just want to see *you*. You don't need to impress them with complicated moves or fancy pole work. You just need to get up there and do what comes naturally."

That took the pressure off. Still, I practiced in our Brooklyn loft the night before my first gig, which was at the Admiral Theatre in

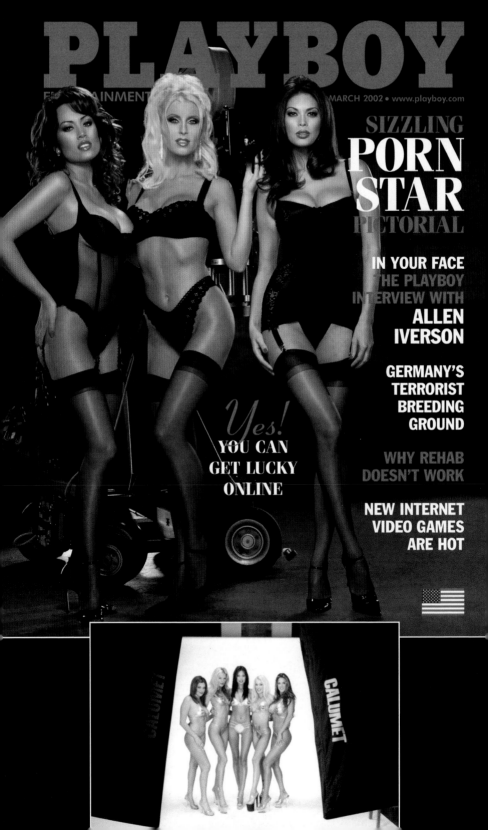

Chicago. I pretended there was a pole and practiced how I would walk around it and what kind of simple little twirls I could do. I just kept reminding myself that if I didn't know what to do, the stripper pole in the middle of that stage would be my safety net. I thought out all of the ways I would use the pole to my advantage: I could hang on it, walk around it holding on with one hand, slide down it with the pole going between my butt, lick the pole seductively, etc. But I had no real routine to speak of. In retrospect, maybe I could've prepared a little more.

Tony Lee just kept reminding me that the fans would love whatever I did, but I couldn't help but wonder: Are they going to expect me to shoot fire out of my ass? What are they going to expect to see? I was terrified but excited before my first show.

We get to my dressing room backstage at the Admiral, and I immediately felt comfortable as I saw photos of Chasey Lain, a gorgeous Vivid Girl, on the wall. I felt like I was in good company and it eased my fears a little bit. I got suited up in a pink/black/white punk-rock schoolgirl outfit and walked out of my dressing room to see what the stage looked like, and I was shocked. It wasn't called Admiral *Theatre* for nothing! The "club" was actually an old theater with theater seating and a traditional stage . . . with *no* stripper pole! I was horrified. I had planned to walk out onstage and head straight to that pole, but this stage didn't have one. What was I going to do? Panic set in. They announce me; my heart starts pounding, and all I can think is, "I have no idea what I'm doing! I didn't plan for a stage without a pole!"

The curtain opened and there were five hundred fans out there all standing up and cheering for me to come out and do my thing. The lights were bright and the crowd was loud and I still didn't know what my first move was going to be. It felt like one of those dreams where you find yourself naked in a classroom and everyone is staring at you. I was petrified. But I knew I couldn't disappoint. So I put on a huge smile and I walked out onstage as if I was walk-

177

ing onto a catwalk and I did my best runway walk. The crowd went crazy and I immediately felt more at ease.

After a few introductory bend-overs and kisses blown to the crowd, my stripper instinct took over and somehow I just knew exactly what to do. Every girl has an inner stripper, and I was no different. Off my clothes went. One by one, I peeled off my lingerie and threw it on the stage like an old pro. It was exhilarating. Every move I made, the crowd cheered me on. I was trying to keep my sexy face on, but I couldn't help but smile. I've never done anything so raw before in front of such a large audience. It was a thrill.

My early shows were more like a photo shoot in slow motion. I would walk around the stage doing various modeling poses to the music. But it was very sexual. The first song was like the foreplay and I'd take off my sheer robe or little top. The second was where the sex begins and I'd take off my skirt or shorts. The third song was the big reveal and off my top would go. And the fourth and final song was the big climax when my panties would come off and I'd do my giveaways of posters and photos.

A typical set-list for my show was:

1. AC/DC, "Girls Got Rhythm"
2. Def Leppard, "Pour Some Sugar on Me"
3. Marilyn Manson, "Great Big White World"
4. AC/DC, "Givin the Dog a Bone"

When my fifteen minutes were up, I ran backstage, pleased with my performance, still panting and hot from the show. Evan rushed in and immediately yelled, "What did you do?"

"What? No, 'Great job on your first show, honey'?" I thought.

"You forgot to take their money!" Evan said.

The bouncer then walks backstage and says to Evan, "Why didn't she take any money?"

Oh my God! They were right. I forgot to take the money from the customers! I was so excited to be onstage performing that I forgot to even one time bend down and take that 20-dollar bill from the guy's hand like you're supposed to. It was flashing back to me now. The stage was lined with girls and guys holding up bills, waving money at me, and looking up at me in anticipation. And I forgot to go to those fans and take their money!

"You did not take one dollar from the customers," Evan sighed, completely exasperated.

No worries. I could make up the loss by selling them my merchandise. I powdered up my face, put on fresh lipstick, and threw on a sexy robe and went out to greet my fans. There were about 300 fans in line waiting to spend their money on me. For $50, they could pose for a Polaroid photo with me topless, and I would sign the photo. For $30, they could buy a signed DVD of one of my movies. And for just $10 they could buy a signed 8 × 10 glossy photo of me. Between the guaranteed fee of $3,000 and my merchandise sales, I made close to $10,000 that night.

But more important, it helped pull me out of my depression because: (1) I had a job and we needed the money. (2) I got to go on a dance tour and see new places. And (3) There is nothing like standing onstage and having a room full of people cheering for you. I felt like a rock star. It was a creative new outlet for me. It's something so terrifying and so freeing at the same time. And dancing turned me on. When the crowd cheered for me, my nipples would get hard and my pussy would get wet. Dancing was another way to turn guys on and be the exhibitionist that I am.

I think dancers are among the bravest people in the world. You are going out onstage whether you feel you look good or not and you are taking money from people. The average person has that nightmare of being in class or in the boardroom and suddenly they are naked, or on a busy street and naked. We live that nightmare. But for me, it was my dream.

Proud of my earnings as a stripper

That dream soon took me dancing all around the world from every major city in the U.S. to France, Germany, Austria, Switzerland, Italy, Belgium, Portugal, Hungary, Croatia, England, Scotland, Australia, and other countries. I made $3,000 for my guaranteed fee at every show, but took in between $10,000 and $60,000 per engagement with the tips (which I never failed to remember to pick up after that first time) and merchandise sales each night. I danced three weekends a month for about four years in a row. The Foxy Lady in Rhode Island was one of my biggest bookings—$35,000 for ten shows. We came home with nearly $60,000 in twenties, tens, fives, and singles that night. The strangest place I danced was at Anthony's Showplace in Tennessee. It was a converted church. As I strutted my stuff onstage I kept saying in my head, "Sorry, God!"

But hands down, the craziest performance I ever danced was on July 24, 2004, at the Pink Pony in Atlanta. I was into my third song, which was either Marilyn Manson's "Great Big White World" or Deftones' "Change," and I do this move where I'm on my back on the floor with my back arched and my legs slightly spread and I do a little shimmy. All of a sudden, I feel this girl right between my legs and she's trying to take my panties off. There was no security, and Evan was off getting the bag of merchandise that I throw out to the crowd for my final song.

I bolted upright and tried to push her way, literally kicking her away with my legs and she's still clinging on to me. I was screaming, "No! No! No!" but kind of laughing at the same time. The girl was clearly wasted and she was just going for it . . . going for *me*! She was relentless and wouldn't let up. I think she just got really excited and couldn't contain it. All of a sudden the DJ says, "Wow. We got a live one!" Evan finally saw what was happening, rushed to my side, and pushed her back down.

One of my favorite dancing gigs was at the Trails Men's Club in Salt Lake City, Utah. It's a gorgeous club with a long, winding stage with rails on the sides that you can really use to your advantage when dancing. And it was a pasties club, which meant that I didn't have to get naked! Once in a while, I liked *not* having to get naked. I felt like a true rock star there. They put a star with my name on it on the outside of my dressing room door and gave me monogrammed towels to use for my shower that night. I still have those towels. And my dressing room was filled with gift baskets of champagne, soaps, perfume, lotions, body sprays, and other girlie things that I loved.

Two very pretty strippers walked in and said, "Hi, Tera. We're really big fans. And we have a little present for you."

"Oh, no," I thought. "Are they going to get naked or something? I'm sooo not a lesbian."

"We heard you love pot, so we got you some marijuana popcorn," they said.

Strippers aren't usually that nice. You know how girls can get.

The only place I didn't feel welcome was in Las Vegas. Vegas is such a strip club town that they don't really need to bring in feature dancers, and when they do, the girls get pretty snippy about it. Such was the case one night at Little Darlings. I didn't ask for this, but the club owners gave me the entire dressing room area instead of just one room. Naturally, this pissed off the regular dancers there. As I was getting ready for my show, I had to listen to strippers bitch loudly, "Tera Patrick has our dressing room. Who does she think she is?"

I'm usually nice to the girls. I always gave them free Polaroids with me and hung out and talked with them. But if these girls were going to be bitchy, well, two can play that game.

I fired back: "That's right, bitch. I have your dressing room. You know what? You get your pussy ripped on set and you can have your own dressing room too!"

Now that we'd become famous, there was terrible gossip about Evan and me in the adult industry trade papers and on gossip sites. They were saying things like Evan got me hooked on heroin and he was just using me to get ahead. Here is this guy who has a crazy fiancée who's been institutionalized, is on medication, had filed for bankruptcy and who he spent all of his money on, and they are saying he's the bad guy? It really hurt me. He treated me so well and I wouldn't be here today if it weren't for his love and support.

The worst rumor was the drug thing. Evan's been sober since August 1, 1988, and I quit drinking for a while the January after I met him, thanks solely to him. I've never done heroin, cocaine, or any hard drug—just Valium when I was young or some pot here and there. But I do still drink, even though I went to AA and spent 2003–2007 sober. AA got me through a period in life where I was abusing alcohol and using it as way to cope or escape. Once I became more stable, I learned that I could control myself and handle a glass of champagne or two with a friend or at a party.

Now would be a good time to set the record straight on the *other* rumors that have plagued my career. . . .

RUMOR VS. TRUTH:

RUMOR: Evan made me get a boob job, dye my hair blond, and get tattoos.

TRUTH: Hell no. If you don't already know by now, I'm a strong-willed woman who makes my own decisions and have been violating my own body of my own free will long before Evan came along. In fact, Evan has never been fond of girls with tattoos. And as for the boob job and dye job, I did those in 2003, which was the roughest year for me. I just wanted to treat myself to something special and make a change. So I got Lasik eye surgery so I didn't have to wear glasses anymore. I always wanted to be a blonde like my idol Marilyn Monroe, so I dyed my hair. And when I first came into the business I was 130 pounds, but when I did *Playboy* in 2002, I lost a ton of weight and dropped down to about 107 pounds and then stayed around 110 for years and I lost some of my boobs. I used to be a full D cup, then I went down to a small D, almost a large C, and I wanted my boobs back, so I got them upped to a DD. It was 100-percent my choice.

RUMOR: I'm half Jewish.

TRUTH: I'm not Jewish, but I got a lot of it in me over the years because Evan is Jewish. I don't practice any one religion. I don't consider myself religious. But I've always been very spiritual and I do believe there is a God. Both of my parents, however, are Buddhist and I do believe in some Buddhist ideas. And as a child, when my parents were still married, I attended Sunday school at a Pentecostal church and loved to sing and read from the Bible.

RUMOR: I worked with Salma Hayek on a USO tour.

TRUTH: I did do a USO autograph signing in January 2002 at Edwards Air Force Base in Mojave, California, but not with Salma Hayek. I never met her, but she has great tits and I would love to meet her someday. That autograph signing was special for me, though. A young military daughter came up to me and said, "I wanted to meet you because when they said your name in the announcement, all of the guys in my section cheered." So I signed to her, "Maybe someday they'll cheer for you too."

RUMOR: I'm a hunter.

TRUTH: Nope. I love animals and have never killed an animal, unless fishing counts. But my dad was a hunter and I would go with him on hunting trips.

RUMOR: Carmen Electra was mad that I used her real name as my professional name.

TRUTH: False. We've actually met, and she was very friendly with me! In fact, this is what she says on the matter: "The first time I heard about Tera Patrick, the porn star, I truly thought that was her real name. When I found out Tera Patrick was inspired to use my name as her porn name, I was flattered. Every time I see her at an awards show or event, Tera is so sweet, beautiful, intelligent, and obviously sexy."

RUMOR: I was a Ford model.

TRUTH: False. I was signed to the Morning Sun Agency in Tokyo, Japan. I was scouted by Ford, which referred me to my agency.

RUMOR: I speak fluent Hungarian.

TRUTH: No. I only speak sexy. But I once had a Hungarian boyfriend and I learned a few Hungarian phrases.

RUMOR: I dated and/or slept with Vin Diesel, Eminem, Gene Simmons, Michael Douglas, Charlie Sheen, Nicolas Cage, and Reggie Miller.

TRUTH: Hell to the Fucking No. Except for the one sexless date with Reggie Miller, the only other celebrity I fucked was the late Alice in Chains lead singer Layne Staley.

RUMOR: I've had gangbangs with a S.W.A.T. team, Navy SEALs, and an entire firehouse.

TRUTH: No gangbangs. Sure, I fucked in *front* of some firemen but I only did the one. I did once confess that I fantasized about filming a gangbang, but I never did it and I think if I did, I would've regretted that big-time!

CHAPTER 20

The Birth of Teravision

Tony Lee was right. I made a ton of money from feature dancing and it more than covered our legal bills. After battling it out in court for most of 2003, we settled with Digital. Steve Hirsch, the owner of Vivid Video, was instrumental in convincing us to settle with Digital.

Steve's interest in me helped me make the decision to settle with Digital. The deal on the table was this: I would be a Vivid Girl, and he would help us with our new company, Teravision, by guiding us and serving as the distribution company for our company's films.

But I still had this thing about settling with Digital. I didn't want it to mean I was backing down. Evan and my lawyer came to me and said, "Listen, you're operating off of emotion right now. If I learned anything from the music industry, it is that I got ripped off on my first album. I signed a really bad deal. You just have to let it go, let the anger go, and take what they give you. You're going to work. You're going to be Tera Patrick."

I agreed to settle on Thanksgiving 2003, and boy did I have a lot to be thankful for. I cooked my first Thanksgiving dinner for

Evan and Sammy, and it was the beginning of a fresh new start in the industry.

I never dreamed of owning my own business until I met Evan. I just didn't think it was something that I could even do if I wanted to. But Evan made me realize how much I was capable of doing if I really wanted to. Just when I was ready to give up, he encouraged me to fight on and made me believe in myself and that I was capable of more. My goal for Teravision was to form a company that produced beautiful movies where the women always looked gorgeous and classy and the performers in it where treated like stars. We were trying to portray women in a positive way. We were also trying to make high-quality films to elevate the business. We had our movies at high price points, and we wanted everyone else to have their movies at high price points to bring us all up.

While I was excited to own my own company and thrilled I could work again and under my name, I still had one hesitation. The big dilemma now was that I didn't really want to do more movies and fuck other men. I was in love, and I just didn't want to have sex with anyone other than Evan. I couldn't do it. Call me old-fashioned, but I only wanted to share my body, my most intimate moments, and myself with my husband.

Evan said to me, "It's great that you won. But what have you won? It doesn't count if you don't now do something with it. Look, for your career, you need to make movies again. Your fans want you to."

"But I don't want to have sex with another man," I told him.

"Well, I don't want you to either," he said.

And then he made the decision that would change everything. "How about if you have sex with *me* on camera?"

"What? Really?" I was surprised. My ex-boyfriend wanted nothing to do with porn, and here was a guy who was willing to fully jump in and be my partner in crime. For the first time in my life, I had a man who wanted to see me be the best I could be and achieve the most I possibly could.

He said that while he wanted to do this for me, he was worried about how it would affect his son. At the time, Evan was also still trying to have a mainstream acting career. After *Oz* was over, he went on many auditions for movies and television roles. His friends who were mainstream actors would tell him that if he did porn, he wouldn't be able to work in mainstream. So Evan had to make a hard decision about what path he wanted his career to go down. As we know, once you take the porn path, there is no turning back.

I was excited at the thought of doing movies with Evan, but in the back of my head I was a little worried at first. Is his head going to get big from this? There's a long history of guys getting into the business through their porn-star girlfriends, and the end isn't usu-

With Evan, my sometime costar

ally pretty. This is what *everybody* warned me about. But we decided we were stronger than that and we'd do this. Evan would become my sole male porn costar and, after a two-year hiatus, I would return to porn. The first film, my comeback movie, would be *Tera Tera Tera*, which was a Teravision/Vivid production. It was also my first hardcore girl-on-girl film and my first film with Evan.

But first Evan needed a porn name. We did the usual formula of using the name of your first pet with the name of the street you grew up on. But Splasher Ocean didn't exactly work. He came up with Spyder Jonez because his nickname was "Spider" because of his huge spider tattoo on his back. I thought it was such a weird coincidence that my nickname as a child was also "Spider" because of my arachnid-looking limbs. For the last name, Jonez, Evan picked that spelling because he said he thought it sounded like a badass guy in a Blacksploitation film.

The only problem now was: How was I going to have sex with my husband on camera? At home, I can be nasty with him and let myself go. There was no one in the room looking at me, judging me. At home with Evan, we're more extreme. I like to be choked and peed on. We like to get out the rope or duct tape and tie each other up. I didn't know how to do it with him on camera and make it believable, because you have to be so mechanical and safe on camera and that is so different from how we are in real life.

For the mainstream porn companies I've worked for, you have to be careful not to cross the obscenity line. For instance, on camera, most mainstream companies don't let you have sex in bondage. You can do bondage, but penetration can't be involved. Well, at home with Evan, sex and bondage go hand-in-hand. On camera, you can't be tied up and penetrated. That's something else we love to do. Choking, of course, is off-limits on camera. Spanking is OK, but it needs to be consensual and you need to give permission on camera that you want to be spanked. I'll never forgot when Evan and I shot *Sex in Dangerous Places* for Teravision, which featured a scene where he tied me up and fucked me. As we were doing the scene, we had our lawyer on the phone giving the director, Paul Thomas, instructions on what I had to say to avoid legal action. I had to acknowledge that I was being tied up and fucked and that I liked it and it was not against my will.

Digital Playground had always wanted me to be a good girl and not the nasty girl I truly was. I was pure vanilla, a pillow queen who lay back and moaned. But that's not who I really was. I found myself sexually through my husband; I discovered what really gives me pleasure and what works for me. I've done things with Evan in the bedroom that I've never done with another man. I let him wrap his hands around my throat, which gives me a head rush and makes an orgasm even better. I never trusted any man to do that before, but I trust Evan. I never let a man pee on me, but I let Evan. It's about submission, trust, and giving yourself freely to someone, and that's a turn-on.

So Evan and I decided that when we made our Teravision movies, I'd do some things I'd never done on camera before, such as having hardcore sex with a woman, engaging in an on-screen orgy, and doing my first real anal scene. It was time to shed my old image and reemerge as a newly sexually empowered femme fatale. But first we had more important engagements to attend to: our wedding.

CHAPTER 21

Hells Angels, Hookers, and Wedding Bells

1/9/04

I tried being a normal bride-to-be, but my mental issues and torment over the Digital Playground lawsuit kept me in crazy land for most of 2003. For the typical bride, the engagement period is full of bridal showers, picking out china patterns, driving bridesmaids crazy with tons of to-do lists, picking music for the wedding, doing seating charts . . . all that stuff you dream about as a little girl. But nothing in my life was typical. I spent my engagement year in a mental ward, throwing shit at the man who loved me, and tearing my hair out. It's a shock that we made it down the aisle at all.

I was the anti-bride anyway. I never really dreamed about the big white frou-frou wedding with all the bells and whistles. I never really thought about the wedding part of getting married. I just thought about the husband part of getting married. I was more excited to promise myself to one man I could love forever and who would love me forever. Evan, on the other hand, wanted the huge New York Jewish wedding with all of our relatives and friends. He had 300 people on his invite list and thought the Brooklyn Botanic Gardens would be the perfect spot for our big white wedding. He even mentioned a horse-drawn carriage!

"Three hundred?!" I was shocked.

"Oh, no. That's three hundred people; they all get a plus-one," he said.

Six hundred people?! "No way! I'm not having that many people at my wedding!" I wanted it to be more intimate, and I never pictured myself in a white wedding dress. Black was more my style.

"But I love you, baby, and I want to shout it from the rooftops!" Evan tried again.

There was no way that was going to happen, so we shelved those wedding plans and forgot about it for a while. We had enough to deal with on the business front with our deal with Vivid and our new company, Teravision. And we were gearing up to attend the AVN Adult Entertainment Expo in Las Vegas in January. It was my first AVN since my saga with Digital, and I needed to show the porn world that I was back.

On the second night of the convention, Evan and I went to a big group dinner at a restaurant in the Hard Rock Hotel. All night long people kept referring to Evan as my husband or to me as his wife.

"Wait, you guys aren't married?" asked some porn chick at the dinner.

"Nope. Not yet. We're engaged," I said.

"Oh my God. You should get married here in Vegas!" she said.

Evan and I just looked at each other, smiled, and didn't think much of it.

Later that night, we went back to our hotel room at the Venetian Hotel, where the AVNs were held, and Evan had this cute, mischievous look in his eye. He pulled me close to him and said, "Well . . ."

"Well what?"

"Well, will you marry me?"

"Of course. I already told you I'd marry you. See this ring on my finger?"

"Maybe that chick had a good idea at dinner. Let's get married here in Vegas," he said.

I honestly hadn't thought of it, but I was on board. "OK, but on one condition," I told him.

"There's a condition?" He looked concerned.

"Yes. The one condition is that I want an Elvis wedding."

"Done!" And with that, Evan opened up the Yellow Pages and started calling around to wedding chapels. We settled on the Little White Wedding Chapel on the Las Vegas Strip because that's the most famous one. It's hosted such celebrity weddings as those of Paul Newman and Joanne Woodward, Bruce Willis and Demi Moore, and more recently Britney Spears and that childhood friend of hers. We had our choice of the $100 Elvis, $75 Elvis, or the cheesy $50 Elvis. We chose the $100 Elvis, who wore a black suit with a gold lamé jacket and black-and-white wing-tipped shoes, and were on our way to get our marriage license that night.

I was not exactly prepared for a wedding that night. I had nothing to wear and no time to go shopping. Luckily, I had packed this sexy black minidress that Evan loved me in. I never thought I'd be married in a $20 cheap dress from a no-name store in Chicago, but that's exactly what I did. Evan put on his black leather pants, leather jacket, and his vintage "gangsta" hat that belonged to his Grandpa Sam, and he looked so handsome.

We started calling our friends to tell them the big news and to invite them to the wedding. My best friend Anneli Adolfsson, the Swedish photographer who had tried to hook Evan and me up years before, lived in Las Vegas so I called her up, got her ass out of bed, and had her come down to be my maid of honor. We also called Alexis Amore and Mercedes, two porn girls in the industry whom I was good friends with, to be in my wedding party as well.

Being a good ol' Brooklyn boy, finding a best man to stand up for him was very important to Evan. He wanted someone special, someone he respected, so he called up his longtime friend Brendan Manning of the Hells Angels. He lived in New York but always came to Vegas for AVN, so he was already in town. Perfect, we thought. Brendan was like a big brother to Evan and he always looked up to him. And Brendan was like the Hells Angels' Hells Angel. When Brendan said yes, Evan said, "That is a seal of approval on our marriage. I feel like our marriage is blessed now."

As Evan and I made our way from our hotel room to our white stretch limo, we ran into tons of fans and friends. Porn people are everywhere during AVN week—in the elevators, in the hallways, in every bar, on the casino floor. You can't blink without seeing someone you know or someone who knows you. As we made our way past the droves of fans and porn peeps, Evan would shout out, "We're getting married!" We were so excited to spread the word that we were telling people to show up at the chapel to see us get married. We must have had about fifty people there, including some strippers, hookers, porn stars, and other random peeps. But we didn't care. We wanted to share our love with anyone who was happy for us.

Our first order of business was to get a marriage license. The chapel told us that we had until midnight to get our license, and we'd need a witness to go with us. Evan ran into Alexis Amore in the lobby of the Venetian, so he asked her to come with us. She was thrilled to help out. On the limo ride over, Alexis joked, "You know, I can be your bachelor party and bachelorette party all in one in the limo." We had a laugh about it. No pre-wedding threesomes for us, though!

Our second order of business was to get a wedding ring for Evan. I had taken off my engagement ring and gave it to him so he would have a ring to put on my finger. But I didn't have a ring to put on his finger. All he had were some rock-and-roll skull rings, but I didn't want to doom our marriage to death by using one of those. So, Evan borrowed a ring from his friend Jonathan Silverstein, who goes by J. Styles in the porn world. He had recently gotten married, so he loaned Evan his ring for the night.

We pulled up in our limo to the Little White Wedding Chapel, and it looked exactly as cheesy as we'd thought it would; we loved it. There was a middle-aged heavyset woman standing in front of two unity candles looking with wide eyes at the motley crew that just walked in. Some of our friends had already arrived and others were trickling in a little past midnight. Along with Brendan, Anneli, Mercedes, and Alexis, our guests included Hells Angels' Pee Wee; our old friend Jason Reyes, who designs our movie box covers and event flyers; Jason's wife, Raffelina; Keith Gordon, who runs Bizarre Video; Perry Margouleff, an old Brooklyn buddy of Evan's who runs a recording studio in Brooklyn; and a bunch of other porn stars, strippers, and two really friendly hookers. One of them said to us, "We don't know you, but you seem so in love so we're so happy for you! You go girl!" She gave me a big sloppy kiss and hug, and it was one of the sweetest moments of the night.

And of course, our special guest was the Elvis Presley imperson-

My impromptu bridal party

ator who sang "Can't Help Falling in Love," "Love Me Tender," and "Viva Las Vegas."

We said our "I Do's" with tears rolling down our faces. Our vows talked about how we would accept each other for who we are as we are, and not for who we hoped the other could be. He accepted me as the porn star that I am, and I accepted him as the perverted rock star that he is. Everything from the past year flashed before my eyes in that moment: my time on tour with him with Biohazard, my time in the mental ward, and my meltdowns over Digital. I just kept thinking what a mess I had been and in spite of all that, this man still vowed to love me. I had this newfound sense of calm. I felt overjoyed and overwhelmed by this love. A lot of people view marriage as two halves coming together as a whole. But for me it felt like me plus Evan was like one plus one equals three.

After the ceremony, we hopped in the limo and hit a chocolate shop on the way back to the Venetian to get some chocolate-covered strawberries. Evan was always so romantic like that. We arrived back at our hotel suite and he had candles lit around the room and we were finally alone. He looked me in the eyes and said, "It's finally just you and me. From the day I met you, I knew it would always be you and me forever. I want to marry you over and over."

Our wedding might have been a far cry from the huge New York wedding that Evan wanted, but it couldn't have been more romantic or perfect for us. And it only cost us $357!

CHAPTER 22

Mr. Kookaburra and Mrs. Barramundi

A s my manager, Evan quickly figured out that there was a huge porn market internationally. He used his knowledge of touring the world with his band, which made more money overseas than Stateside, and set out to make Teravision and Tera Patrick global brands. Before we knew it, I was appearing at porn conventions and doing my feature dancing show all over the world.

One of the biggest conventions I ever did was the Sexpo in Sydney, Australia, in 2004. I appeared at the convention for a whopping fee of $20,000 (and first-class airfare and accommodations, no less!), but where we really made bank was when they booked me to dance at a venue that normally hosts big rock bands and seats eight thousand people. I had eight nearly sold-out shows in four days there.

Before we knew how big the venue really was and that it was sold out, Evan gave me this pep talk: "Don't worry if there's only two hundred people there. You're new to the market. Don't worry." And then we show up and there were thousands of people there. Once again there wasn't a stripper pole on the stage because it wasn't a strip club, so we decided to improvise a bit and use a chair in the center of the stage as a prop. But that didn't help much. The huge stage made our tiny chair look like Stonehenge from the movie *This Is Spinal Tap*. We were cracking up over that. Evan decided to just treat it like a rock show and use the video monitors at the venue to show my performance. That did the trick.

The large crowd didn't freak me out at all. In fact, it's easier to perform for a larger audience than a more intimate one. It's easy to be great when you have thousands of people screaming for you. The intensity of the crowd really got me going, and I killed!

The line for photos and merchandise afterward was the longest line I'd ever had in my entire career. It was so long and so slow that Evan got a megaphone and was walking down the line telling people, "Due to the large volume of fans, we are selling one thing. It's

Onstage at Sexpo

a package with a DVD, a Polaroid with Tera, and an autographed eight-by-ten photo for fifty Australian dollars." He was embarrassing me. He'd stand up on the table and shout out: "Cash only!"

We sold out of everything, making more than $40,000 in merchandise sales! We had Tera Patrick T-shirts that looked like the Harley-Davidson logo, but they said Tera Patrick and Teravision on them, along with trucker hats, posters, and glossy photos. We were taking in so much cash that Evan had to send a runner out to buy him a fanny pack to put the money in. People joke about "suitcase pimps"—you know, the boyfriend of the porn star who rolls her suitcase around for her, collects (and spends) her dough, and pimps her out. Evan was my fanny-pack pimp on this trip!

We made so much money from this trip that we decided to spend the cash on a lavish vacation in the most exclusive resort in the area: the Hayman Island Resort in the Great Barrier Reef. It's what they like to call a "six-star" resort on a private, remote island. We had to take two flights and two ferries to get there. It's very exclusive and very expensive, but we were busting at the seams with cash and needed a getaway. It was so upscale that when we'd come out of a secluded lagoon after skinny-dipping, there was a butler greeting us with, "Would you care for a towel, madame? How about water, sir?" We didn't think *the Seinfelds* fit in here, so we started addressing each other as Mr. Kookaburra and Mrs. Barramundi. Kookaburra is a bird native to Australia that is known as "the laughing bird" for its loud call, and a barramundi is a native fish. Throughout the entire trip it was, "Good morning Mr. Kookaburra. Would you care for a stroll on the beach today?" "Why yes, Mrs. Barramundi, that sounds like a delightful idea."

We were having the time of our lives in the most beautiful place we'd ever been, so we decided to get married again. Evan said on our first wedding night that he wanted to marry me over and over again, and he made good on that just eight months later. And like Vegas, Evan handled all of the arrangements. He loved whipping up

On the beach at Hayman Island

romantic surprises for me. He went out and got me a diamond wedding band, as I still didn't have a band from our first wedding. A vintage white Rolls-Royce drove us to the ceremony spot on a grassy area elevated above the beach with a stunning view of the water.

I'll never forget Evan's vows to me. He said, "I have no doubt that we will love each other forever. Our life is moving very fast externally, but I just want you to know that, internally, I'm standing still with you, holding hands."

THE RULES OF OUR MARRIAGE:

1. Agree to agree
2. Let the other live out all of their fantasies on camera and off

3. Treat each other's feelings with the utmost care and respect

4. Never forget that our relationship is about love, friendship, fun, compassion, trust, partnership, and, of course, sex

5. When having sex with other people, never forget that it's just about sex

6. Tera is number one to Evan and Evan is number one to Tera

CHAPTER 23

Bye-Bye, Vanilla Girl of Porn

I was up worrying the whole night before our first day of shooting *Tera Tera Tera* on February 2, 2004. This was going to be Evan's first movie. I knew he'd be able to maintain an erection and I knew he'd look hot on camera, but I also knew that fucking on camera is not the same as fucking at home. The advice I gave him was this: "Just remember that you're having sex with your wife, and I'm here to help you in any way I can. Listen to the director, forget about the cameras, and focus on me."

Every newcomer to porn is worried that he won't be able to keep his dick hard for the entire shoot. But Evan didn't have to worry about that. I knew that he'd been able to stay hard for hours with me at home. And even if he did get nervous on the set, I was there to be his "fluffer." There's this myth in porn of girls called fluffers whose only job is to keep the male performer hard in between takes. Maybe it was true back in the day, but today we don't have these extra girls hanging around. It's up to the female performer if she wants to help the guy out or not. If you're nice, you'll suck him off or jerk him off or play with your pussy to keep him aroused. But many girls in porn today are like, "Keep your own dick hard. No one's keeping me wet. It's your problem." I was never one of those girls—I always helped the guy out between scenes. I'd always ask him what turned him on and then I'd do it. I was a giver.

So I told Evan that I would be his fluffer and help him throughout the shoot if he needed it. He wasn't worried about having sex in front of people because, like me, Evan is an exhibitionist.

But he did put some thought into his load. In porn, guys get competitive about how big of a load they can shoot. What makes a great cum shot, you ask? Lots of it! So Evan went to porn star Peter North, who is renowned for having one of the best cum shots in the industry, never failing to deliver a tremendous load. Evan wanted to make sure his wad was worthy too, so he rang up Peter and asked what he does to get such volume. Peter told him that he takes a combination of Chinese herbs with reishi mushrooms and guarana. It didn't sound good to Evan, so he decided to go au naturel.

I could tell he was nervous. I could see it in his face. I'd never seen him nervous before, so he made me a little nervous too. Everyone on set wanted to make sure Evan was comfortable and ready. Our director, a fabulously flamboyant drag queen named Chi Chi LaRue, pulled Evan aside and said, "Do you want some Viagra? Most guys take some type of dick pills."

"No way," said Evan. "I don't mess with that stuff. I'm not going to try it for the first time on my first scene. I'll be fine."

It was time for our first scene: I'm lying on a wooden table in this industrial loft in downtown L.A. in pink lingerie with this huge jeweled necklace on. Evan takes one look at me and says, "Wow. You look so beautiful." Right then, I knew everything would be OK. Here I was doing something again that I love, with the man I love. It felt special. It felt new again. I realized then how much I'd missed it, and I loved being able to share it with him.

We start out by kissing, and then he starts eating my pussy and he's getting into it and I'm getting into it. All is going well and we're both beginning to forget about the cameras and crew and just focus on each other. Just as we are hitting our stride, Chi Chi starts going,

"Yeah. Eat that pussy. Suck that pussy. Let me see that demon hand!" (Evan has a tattoo of a demon on his left hand.) "Put that demon hand in that pussy. Yay!" I'm trying hard not to laugh so I didn't blow the moment, but Evan couldn't take it anymore. Evan stops eating me out and scolds Chi Chi: "Chi Chi," he said, "I love you, but you're making me nervous. Stop talking!"

So Chi Chi and the whole set gets quiet, and we continue the scene. It's moving along nicely and then we hear a stern whisper, "Chopper! Get out of there, Chopper. Chopper, come here!" Chi Chi is trying to get my little dog out of the shot because he'd just walked right into the scene. I start laughing, but Evan's not having it so we have to stop again.

As Evan promised, he had no problem keeping his dick hard or really getting into the scene. In fact, once we started fucking, he was so into it that we had to stop a few times because he was going to cum, but it was too soon for the cum shot. He was so excited that we had to stop a few more times, which was really flattering to me.

"Get me some chocolate!" my rock-hard hubby asked the set assistant. I guess chocolate was a good distraction for the task at hand, and it gave him a little boost of energy . . . not that he needed it. Luckily, this scene didn't have to be shot in one long take. It was our film, our pace, our direction. We could start and stop as often as we needed to, which we did until an hour later when we finished our scene.

"Good job!" cheered Chi Chi, proud of his new porn pet.

Evan was so relieved, he sat down and ate a whole bag of chocolate and declared, "I want to do it again!" He was proud, and I was proud of him.

The reason Chi Chi is my favorite director is because he not only gets the technical angles right—open up to camera, arch your back, point your toes, lean back, etc.—but he's also very concerned with beauty. He makes sure your fake eyelashes aren't crooked or falling off. He makes sure your body makeup is even and glowing and that your lipstick isn't all over your face or that your eyeliner hasn't smudged. He's always looking out for the girl, to make sure he's making the most glamorous and beautiful movie he can make. That's the one thing I took with me when I started Teravision: Always make it glamorous and beautiful. I wanted to leave behind a legacy and it was important for me, like it is for Chi Chi, to make a higher standard of movie than what's out there. And I think we achieved that.

With the first scene in the can, it was time for the most pivotal scene of the movie for me—my first hardcore girl-on-girl scene. You have to understand, all "firsts" in porn are a big deal when you are a big deal. Your first girl scene, your first anal scene, your first DP scene (though I don't do double penetration, but you get the point) is anticipated, talked about, reviewed, scrutinized, and discussed ad nauseam. So we put a lot of time and thought into my first girl hardcore sex scene (which includes penetration and not just oral sex like I did in *Aroused*) since we knew how much attention it would get and that my fans had been waiting for me to do this for five years. For the sake of my career and for this comeback to really make a splash, it had to be exceptional.

I was comfortable with girls. I didn't mind kissing, touching, or having my pussy licked. But I had a fear of going down on a pussy. That was one thing that made me the "vanilla girl of porn," and it was time to shed that image.

Evan knew how important it was for my career as well, and he was my manager, so I listened to his opinions with an open mind. "You have to be with a girl. For one, it'll be hot. For another, it's great for your career," he'd tell me. I agreed with him wholeheartedly and was ready to dive into new territory. Being at the top of my game, I had my pick of the litter, so to speak. I could've picked any pussy I wanted, and I gave it a lot of consideration.

I chose Savanna Samson. I picked her because I found her extremely attractive and she was the opposite of me. She had blond hair, hazel eyes, and was a petite 5' 5". She looked like a hot all-American cheerleader. But more important than her beauty, I chose her because I knew she was really into women and was very experienced. She was a total professional and just loved to fuck. That made me feel more comfortable, because my worst nightmare would've been to be in a cold, sterile scene with a woman who was just doing it for the paycheck and not because she really enjoyed herself. We call that "gay for pay." And as we know, one of my rules of porn is: don't do anything you don't totally love. And I think it was exciting for Savanna, too, because I was going to lose my "vagina virginity" to her.

The other reason I chose her was because I trusted her with my man, and she had a lot of respect for me, Evan, and our marriage. And that was very important to me because it wasn't just me and Savanna getting it on in the movie, there was also a threesome with Evan, and Evan and I had never done a threesome before. I was a bit hesitant about sharing my man with another woman, because I still had a bit of a jealous streak in me at this time, so I wanted to make sure that we did it with a girl who wasn't going to try to steal him away from me. I felt safe with Savanna, and I needed that security blanket to ease my nervousness about this brand-new sexual territory for me.

Before we got to the threesome, Savanna and I had our scene together. I couldn't believe I was about to have real sex with a woman for the first time! I was really excited and surprised that I had gone this long without ever going there. But I was also really nervous because I didn't really know how to lick pussy. The stuff I'd done in magazines was pretty fake. Now it was time for Evan to give me some advice: "Do what feels good to you. Touch her the way you want to be touched. She'll help guide you, and it will become instinctual before you know it."

From the shooting script of *Tera Tera Tera:*

LIVING ROOM FLOOR IN FRONT OF FIREPLACE

SEX SCENE WITH TERA AND SAVANNA

CHANGE OF SCENE

TERA STANDING ON STAIRCASE

> TERA: Mum, well, I'd like to get a little crazy for this next scene . . . and nothing would turn me on more than to see seven hard, luscious bodies all fucking and sucking one another. [SHOWING STILLS OF GROUP] Three big, hard beautiful cocks and four wet sticky pussies. I'd like to watch the cocks slide in and out of those wet pussies and I'd like to see tongues . . . long tongues running all over bodies . . . Hum, and big luscious lipstick lips wrapped around big hard cock . . . all those big hard cocks being sucked. . . . Oooh I'd love to suck a cock after it's been in another woman's pussy. I love to taste that juice . . . ahhh, I like to see it go in a mouth, in a pussy with those hot lights beating down on all those sweaty bodies . . . making them hotter and hotter.

TERA STARTS TO PLAY WITH HERSELF

> TERA: All those juicy cum shots on all those pretty faces . . . I want to lick that cum . . . I love licking cum off faces . . . oohh, I wish this pussy was filled right now . . . feel me, feel me, taste me . . . fuck me . . .

CHANGE OF SCENE

Chi Chi didn't tell me this until later, but he was freaking out over this scene. There was a lot riding on it: Tera Patrick's First Hardcore Girl Scene! He told Evan that his biggest fear was that I would chicken out and make Savanna do all of the work. He thought I would just lie there and be the pillow queen that I usually was and not get into it. And for the scene to work, it was imperative that I really got into it.

Savanna was having a glass of wine before the scene to relax, and for the first time in almost a year, I really, really wanted a drink. But I had been sober and was sticking with sobriety, so I kept myself away from the vino. The setup for the scene was so relaxing and inviting anyway that I didn't need any wine. We were in front of a cozy fireplace with tons of pillows around, and once Chi Chi yelled, "Action!" I surprised myself at how comfortable and relaxed I felt.

We started out caressing each other's breasts. She felt so soft and smooth. That's one thing I love about women: the softness of their skin and the sexy curves of their bodies. She had a gentle touch and knew just how to make me tingle. Her eyes were magnetic and, in the moment, I just fell in love with her. Savanna had a womanly body with real curves and soft flesh—unlike the hard, overly worked-out bodies on some of the younger girls. I don't like to feel muscles on a girl. I like to feel some flesh.

We began kissing and I remember loving how moist and soft her tongue felt. It was so sensual. Kissing a girl is a lot different from kissing a guy. It's more sensual and loving. We kissed slowly and gently. It wasn't what I expected in a porn scene. I was getting very turned on and all of a sudden, Evan was right: It became instinctual and as Savanna got into doggy-style position, I went right up behind her and started licking her pussy. She smelled fresh and clean. My instincts took over and I buried my face and tongue in her pussy and threw myself into it as she moaned and writhed with pleasure. And to my surprise, I really loved it. It turned me on more than I thought it would.

Chi Chi just couldn't shut up, though. He started going, "Yes, Tera! Yes, Tera! Oh my God, Tera. Good girl, Tera!" I looked over at him at one point and he was literally pulling his hair, saying, "This is so beautiful!" Then Chi Chi winked at me, and that gave me all the confidence I needed. I wanted to not just please Savanna, but I wanted to make my favorite director happy too.

Not as happy as Evan, though. Evan had always wanted to see me with a girl. I mean, that's every guy's fantasy, right? Like any hot-blooded male, seeing two girls get it on was a huge turn on for Evan. Out of the corner of my eye I could see Evan standing right behind the camera in the monitor, rubbing his dick with a smile on his face as Savanna and I went at it. Evan had this look on his face like, "I am going to fuck the hell out of you later, girl!" I couldn't wait for that.

It was finally time for my first threesome with Evan and Savanna. I was so against threesomes. I just never wanted to share my man with another woman. I was so sure that no one could ever come between us, but I still didn't want to share him. So, like I said before, when it comes to threesomes, the key to a happy and healthy ménage à trois is to set up some boundaries and make sure all parties adhere to them.

My boundaries were the following: Evan couldn't fuck Savanna. Evan couldn't go down on Savanna. What Evan could do was touch her, put his fingers in her, and let her give him a blowjob. That was it. His cock was not going into any other woman's pussy . . . period.

Savanna completely respected our rules and was totally cool about it. The threesome scene went great. I ate her out, she ate me out, we both gave Evan the blowjob of his life, and all was great. Evan was so turned on that when he stood up to blow his big load on both of our faces, he overshot. And I mean he *really* overshot and hit the camerawoman from clear across the room—about ten feet. Evan felt really bad. And even though he was impressed with his Olympic "pop shot," he wished it had stayed on the person it was meant for.

After the shoot, Evan was on a mission to get stronger—"stronger" for porn guys means to be able to last longer. He thought, well, practice makes perfect. So every night after our four-day shoot, we'd go back home and he'd fuck the shit out of me to practice lasting longer. He really worked hard at being the best porn performer he could be. We'd be tired from a long day on set, but he was up for the challenge.

"We gotta fuck more!" he'd say.

"Evan! You're killing me! I can't even walk." But I always succumbed to his charms. I mean, I loved fucking my husband and I wanted him to be the best performer he could be too.

In front of the billboard in L.A. announcing Tera, Tera, Tera

It was a really exciting time. I was so happy to be making movies again and thrilled to be doing it with Evan. But what made it even more empowering was that we were doing it for our company, our dream, and our own profits. We were the ones to really win out this time, and that felt great.

Evan and I had the perfect plan. I was going to only work with Evan for a couple of years, make as many movies in that time as I felt comfortable making, and then stop making movies but have them released for years to come so I would still technically be active in the porn industry. I just wanted to get all the porn out of the way so I could spend time enjoying the fruits of my lusty labors over the years, which included doing glamorous magazine shoots, writing for *Genesis* magazine, making personal appearances, feature dancing, and doing television appearances. I basically wanted to enjoy being a star, and didn't plan to spend the next several years on end filming movie after movie. I wanted to film a lot now, put them in the can, and let them roll out for years to come. And of course, this plan entailed fucking only my husband on-screen and doing the occasional half-assed threesome with him where I get to play all I want but he needs to keep his dick out of the other woman. This plan worked out just fine for all of 2004 and 2005.

Having my own company afforded me the opportunity to make some dreams come true for my husband and me. For me, I always wanted to do a strong, female-empowering film with an all-Asian cast so that I could really embrace my ethnic background and help out some other Asian girls in the industry in the process. I am proud of being half Thai, and I wanted to celebrate that with a sexy film filled with a bevy of sexy Asian babes of all shapes, sizes, and backgrounds. I had never done an all-Asian movie of my own, and this was a way to give back to my community and to please my Asian fans. For my perverted, horny husband who likes Asian women, this worked out too.

So in June 2004, we made both of our dreams come true when

we shot *Reign of Tera*, which would become the most popular and bestselling film of my career. Evan wrote the script, which centered on me as the madam of this Asian love palace, which was a place where men would come and be worshiped and fucked by hot Asian girls. I handpicked the girls for the movie myself, including my old friend Charmane Star, as well as Lucy Thai, Lily Thai, Kianna Dior, Jade Hsu, Jayna Oso, Nyomi Marcela, Nautica Thorn, Mika Tan, Veronica Lin, and others. My dog Chopper also made his feature-film debut in *Reign of Tera* (not in a sex scene, though!).

We went all out for *Reign of Tera*. It was our first big-budget production for Teravision, and we paid attention to every little detail. I even had outfits custom made for all of the girls and even for Chopper. We had special sets built and found authentic ancient gongs to use in some scenes.

Reign of Tera featured my first orgy scene. It was yet another way to show off the new Tera. The scene featured me, Evan, and a bunch of the girls in the movie all in a bed, having sex with one another. My rule was still in place, though: No fucking other girls for Evan! He could only get his dick sucked. It was one big Asian free-for-all. I was fucking Evan. I was fucking girls. Girls were fucking one another. Girls were dildoing one another. One girl even had her foot in another girl's pussy. It was crazy sex! We were all laughing and moaning and squealing with delight. This was Evan's dream come true.

I felt on top of the world in that moment. It was really an empowering movie for me. I wasn't just playing the role of this strong, confident, powerful, in-charge lady boss on top in the movie, but in real life as owner of Teravision, I was actually the strong, confident, powerful, in-charge woman on top. I finally felt like I was holding all the cards for once. In the moment of shooting this film, I felt like something magical was happening, and I was right. To this day, it's the movie I'm most known for.

The next important film I made was *Teradise Island: Anal Fever*. It was important because it was my first true anal scene, and it's rare to have the career I had without ever doing a scene like this. I say first "true" anal scene because as some of my hardcore fans will know, I did a small, low-budget film early in my career where a guy put his penis in my butt for a brief moment, but it wasn't a full-fledged anal sex scene. There's a big difference between a small little poke in the butt and the full-on anal pounding that I got in *Anal Fever*, so most of my fans and I consider this movie to be my true first anal film.

Evan was thinking strategically about my career. If we were going to reinvent me as a nastier, more hardcore version of myself, then giving my fans a proper, fully realized anal scene was definitely the next step.

We shot *Teradise Island: Anal Fever* and *Teradise Island 2* over a one-week period in Maui, Hawaii, in August 2005. I figured if I was going to do anal, I might as well be doing it in a tropical paradise. And I was excited that I'd be doing my first filmed anal with my husband. I wouldn't have it any other way. I loved surrendering myself to him, and I knew we'd shoot it in a really beautiful way.

But it wasn't an easy shoot. We shot on the beach at five in the morning and it was a bit chilly. Evan had a tough time staying hard at first because of the cold, sand was going up both of our cracks, and I was lying on these rocks for part of the scene, so it was difficult to get comfortable. But we nailed it.

Now that we were about a year into doing movies together, I was feeling a little more secure with Evan being a porn star. I started letting go of my old hang-ups with him and let him, for the first time, lick another girl's pussy in this movie. It was a scene with Alexis Amore, and I wouldn't let him fuck her, but I did let him go down on her. She was a good friend of mine, and I knew I could trust that she wouldn't try to steal my husband and I was beginning to trust that Evan wasn't going to leave me. The more open Evan and I got with our rules, the better our films were.

On the set of Teradise Island

The next day after we shot those scenes, Evan and I snuck off and had a really nice romantic lovemaking session on the beach in the middle of the night. It was great to go from our hardcore, raunchy sex scenes for the movie to real, tender lovemaking in our real life. We had such a great sexual balance and were both fulfilling every fantasy we ever had.

CHAPTER 24

Back to My Roots

One night in bed Evan said to me, "You know what? You're a porn star. And porn stars don't only fuck their husbands on camera. It's not that I want to share my wife with any-one, but I know you love me and I know it would be just for our business. I think you should start doing other guys again on film."

I didn't know if he was the most selfless husband in the world or the craziest. What man wants his woman to do other guys? At first I was like, "No way. I just don't want to sleep with another man. I'm married to you. I only want you."

I wasn't ready to share myself. Here I was with my husband, enjoying being married. We'd just had the best sex, we had the best of everything, and now he was telling me that I needed to bang other guys. In my mind there wasn't one guy I wanted to fuck in the business. Been there, done that.

I didn't want to question Evan wanting me to work with other men again, because it's different in porn. He knows and I know that having sex on camera is just work. It's just another day at the office for us. It wasn't like I was picking up some hot guy at Quizno's and saying, "Hey baby, wanna fuck?" You have a different mind-set when you work in porn. And even though on an intellectual level I knew that, deep down I was emotionally torn over it.

But I gave it some thought and I agreed that my fans were getting bored of seeing me fuck my husband movie after movie. It was time for me return to my roots and be the full-fledged porn star who does everyone and (almost) everything. The problem was that at the time I didn't think there were any cute guys with big dicks who I'd be attracted to in the industry.

"Baby, you can choose any guy in the world that you want to work with," Evan reminded me.

I was worried about betraying my husband. I worried that I was going to do it and he was going to be angry with me because he was a little insecure about me doing it. As much as he was trying to talk me into it, he could be jealous sometimes too. Jealousy is natural, of course, when you're talking about your wife fucking another guy. He was like, "I don't really want to share my woman with anybody, but I trust you and I love you, and your fans will love this."

We spent days looking through some porn websites to find me the right guy. I wasn't too picky, but I did want a guy who was taller than me. I decided on Tommy Gunn. Tommy Gunn is from New Jersey and he looks it, showing off the guido look to full effect. He is a real macho guy with short spiky brown hair, tanned skin, and usually some sort of facial hair like a goatee. More important, he has a rock-hard body and a pretty big dick—eight inches to be exact. He looked good to me, and it didn't hurt that he was one of the most popular guys in the industry at the time, all of the girls liked him, he had a good reputation, and Evan trusted him.

Steve Hirsch at Vivid chose the second guy in the film: Jean Val Jean. He was a six-foot-two French guy with long, flowing, Fabio-like hair and a model-esque face. He was a little too pretty for me, but he worked great for the movie because he was tall, handsome, and made the director, Paul Thomas, happy.

Steve already had a movie in mind for me to do: *Tera Patrick's*

Fashion Underground, a feature film where I was a supermodel and the head of my own modeling agency. It was to be my next big Vivid/Teravision movie for 2006. We shot it on January 13, 2006, and I got paid a lot of money for it. It ended up winning an AVN Award for Best Cinematography.

To make it more comfortable for both of us, the director of the film, Paul Thomas, was going to let Evan direct the boy-girl scene instead of Paul doing it himself. Actually, when I think about it, having Evan direct the scene was easier for Evan, but it actually made me nervous as hell. It was weird enough to be fucking another guy for the first time in four years, yet another thing to have my husband in the room watching, but having him behind the camera directing us on what to do was a bit unnerving.

The first position we filmed was doggy-style, and I was getting into it and trying to ignore the fact that my husband was right there. As Tommy and I were fucking, I turned around to look at him and I kissed him. Out of the corner of my eye, I saw Evan's face drop. He was like, "Whoa." I didn't even think that a kiss would affect him more than fucking, but when you think about it, kissing and fucking don't always go together. "Oopsie," I thought.

Then I hear Paul Thomas say to Evan, "Wow. I guess she really is into it." Evan looked a little disturbed, so for the rest of the scene, I made sure not to kiss Tommy again. Actually, I felt weird through-out the rest of the scene, like I was holding back a little.

When the scene was over and I was in my dressing room, I saw Evan walking up the stairs toward my dressing room. He announced loudly to everyone to clear the set and looked mad as hell. I thought he was going to scream at me for something. But instead, he didn't say a word. He just took off his clothes, grabbed me forcibly, and fucked the hell out of me. I guess he had to mark his territory. And it creeped me out to see him that jealous and take such control.

We talked about it afterward and he was like, "You kissed him. You kissed him." Kissing is very intimate, so I agreed never to kiss another performer again. He never brought it up again. He said that he didn't want to hold me back as a performer, but kissing was off limits.

I definitely had a hard time getting through the rest of the movie. My scene with Jean Val Jean was really cold. I didn't get close to him. I wasn't really into the scene. But at the end of the day, Evan and I were on the same page about what was needed for my career and what would be best for Teravision. And Evan had had to make some hard, selfless decisions that ended up paying off big-time in terms of us growing our business . . . and our bank accounts.

I was really proud of the work I was doing with Vivid and Teravision. It felt like the drama with Digital Playground was light years behind me. I felt relieved, but I also felt a sense of vindication. I won. I was able to not just be successful on my own, but to find even greater heights of success and satisfaction by doing it my way. I could do porn, be in love, and have it all. Sinner takes all!

Chapter 25

Three Awful Weeks

"Chopper's been kidnapped!" I cried into the phone to Evan as I stood shaking outside our Cadillac Escalade with the door wide open. My six-pound black-and-white fox terrier dog, Chopper, and his carrying bag were missing.

"Get here now!" I wailed.

I couldn't believe what just happened. I was running into the Westfield Fashion Square Mall in Sherman Oaks for just a few minutes, and I left Chopper in the car alone. Big mistake. I don't know if I forgot to lock the door of if I hit the Lock button but it didn't work, but when I walked out of the mall and approached my car, my heart sunk as I saw the door wide open and my little baby nowhere to be found.

Evan was used to getting 911 calls from me for a variety of reasons, but usually it was because I went shopping by myself without a bodyguard or assistant and ended up being trapped by fans or autograph-seekers and couldn't deal with it. But this 911 call was a *real* emergency, and Evan dropped what he was doing and rushed over to the mall. It was useless looking around the parking lot because I knew Chopper was kidnapped. Someone took him. I immediately thought maybe it was an enemy of mine or maybe it was even a fan because I put Chopper in some of my movies and we did photo shoots with him. So, maybe someone knew it was my dog and took him for a ransom. Evan immediately sprang into action. As I cried and hyperventilated, he went through the security tapes with the mall guards.

I bonded with Chopper like you bond with your firstborn. As someone who didn't have or want children at the time, my dogs were my babies; and Chopper was my first. (Mr. Big Time, a teacup Chihuahua; and Bandit, a Dutch shepherd, came next.) I took Chopper everywhere with me—to the set, to shoots, to dinner, on vacation, when I travel. He was my constant companion. I was devastated when I saw the car and him not sitting there waiting for me.

Everything stopped and Evan put everyone at Teravision— especially Robert Mora, my assistant, and Maxx Padilla, our VP—on the job of finding Chopper. Teravision production stopped, I canceled all of my work, and for three long weeks we had teams of people looking for Chopper. And for three whole weeks I didn't sleep a wink.

We even called our publicist at the time, Lizzie Grubman, and did a full-court press on it. She got me on every radio show on Sirius radio, on KTLA TV in L.A., on *The Howard Stern Show*, in *New York Post*'s Page Six, and other media outlets so I could let people know we were offering a $5,000 reward for my baby. We also put ads in every newspaper we could think of, including the *Los Angeles Times*, *The Daily News*, the *LA Weekly*, *Star* magazine, and Spanish publications like *La Opinion*.

I asked Evan to call his biker buddies, street gang members, and even guys with ties to the Mexican mafia—who, according to Evan, know everything that goes down on every street in L.A.—to comb the streets looking for Chopper. We even hired street teams of people to pound the pavement for us. We signed up for every dog-search service we could find, such as Sherlock Bones, FidoFinder .com, and Home Again.

Within the first hour of Chopper going missing, we had four-color flyers made up and started posting them from the Valley into Hollywood and all the way to Downtown L.A. and other surrounding areas. We spent thousands of dollars looking for Chopper, and lost tens of thousands in the work we missed for those three weeks.

I was beside myself. I was sleeping with Chopper's leash around my neck, crying myself to sleep, and even walking the neighborhood at night in my bathrobe with a flashlight looking for Chopper under parked cars. Evan and everyone really thought I was heading for another breakdown and would end up in the psych ward again. It was awful.

Fans were sending flowers, cards, and gifts of condolences to the offices. Evan had already begun looking for a new dog to get for me. He was convinced Chopper was dead or off with another family and never coming back. But I kept saying, "He's coming home. I just know it." They thought it was crazy.

I couldn't eat. I couldn't shower. I couldn't put makeup on. I certainly couldn't work. But around the third week of the big Chopper search, after everyone else had given up hope, I finally pulled myself together enough to make a personal appearance at a party during the Pro Bowl in Hawaii that I was booked for. The night before I left for the trip, I went on *The Howard Stern Show* to make one last plea for the return of Chopper and to remind people that we would give a $5,000 reward with no questions asked.

I'll never forget our last day in Hawaii. I was on my phone with my sister Debby, crying about Chopper. I was calling Debby every day during this time and sometimes at two or three in the morning. And my sister got serious with me and said, "Linda, you just have to let him go. It's been three weeks. Just think of him as this little angel who came down to live with you for a short while, and let him go." I hung up the phone with her, and Evan got a call from Robert.

"We got him," Robert told Evan.

"You have Chopper?" Evan couldn't believe it.

"We don't have him yet, but we got a call and I believe it's him."

Evan was skeptical because we received many other calls from people saying they had Chopper but it never ended up being Chopper. We hopped on the next flight back to L.A., and Robert was right. It was Chopper. Two Armenian lesbians from the Valley had the dog. It was a "no questions asked" deal, so we never did get the full details of how or why Chopper was abducted. But Robert gave them the check for $5,000 and got Chopper back. The Armenians told him that they renamed the dog Prince because he pranced around like he was royalty and because he looked like a pygmy, kind of like the artist Prince.

We got Chopper back on Valentine's Day 2005, two years from when Evan gave him to me, and it was the best Valentine's Day ever. It just proved that if you don't give up, the unthinkable might come true. I knew Chopper would come back to me, and he did. I squeezed him so hard and never left him alone again.

Oh, and, when we got home from getting Chopper back, Evan tried to cancel the $5,000 check, but it was too late.

CHAPTER 26

The Power of Tera

Working with Evan as my manager, my costar, and the CEO of my company was starting to really pay off. On a personal level, it brought us even closer together. On a business level, all of the moves that he made—from lining up my feature dancing gigs to the deal with Vivid to encouraging me to expand my sexual horizons on film—led to my big crossover year in 2006. This was the year Evan vowed to take me from top of the porn world to the mainstream world.

When I entered the adult industry, it was not my goal to become a mainstream actress or star. If that's what I wanted to do, I would've gone the typical route of taking acting lessons, going in for auditions, and trying to get bit parts like every Hollywood hopeful does. But that wasn't my quest. I'll be honest, I just wanted to be famous and I liked to model and to be nude. Porn was satisfying. But once the idea of mainstream popularity started becoming more of a possibility, I was pretty excited at the non-adult-industry opportunities that started coming my way.

Evan's first mission was to get me on the cover of a major mainstream magazine. Evan set his sights on *FHM*. It was hip and known for its sexy covers and classy spreads. He worked those *FHM* editors for months, letting them know what I was up to and dragging me out to every *FHM* party so I could network with the magazine and be seen on their red carpets. Finally, one day we got the call. They wanted to shoot me. But at first, I thought it was just another one- or two-page feature. I had no idea it would be for the cover and that I would be the only porn star to ever grace the cover of *FHM*! That was a *huge* deal.

I shot the *FHM* cover on January 30, 2006, at Quixote Studios in Studio City. What a way to kick off the year. About a month after the shoot, Evan got the call from the editor at *FHM* who told him, "Guess what? It's going to be our July cover." When Evan told me, I couldn't believe it. He said *FHM* felt that the photos were just too good not to use—I'd have the cover plus an eight-page spread in the magazine. I went to bed that night with the biggest smile on my face and gave my husband the sex of his life as a thank-you. The *FHM* cover and the *Playboy* cover from 2002 are the two proudest moments of my career.

Even though Evan and I proved that I could be successful in life after Digital Playground, landing this cover really nailed it for me. Every little bit of mainstream success I would get, I thought of it as a big "fuck-you" to Digital, and that felt good. It further proved that I could do it on my own, and that was the best feeling ever.

I couldn't believe how many people came out for my signings of the cover, which had the headline THE POWER OF TERA, at the Virgin Megastore in Times Square on June 19 and the Virgin Megastore at Hollywood and Highland in L.A. the next day. I'd done many signings at porn conventions and adult video stores, but I had never done a mainstream store like Virgin and wasn't quite sure what to expect. My fans didn't disappoint, coming out by the hundreds. To my surprise, there were a lot of fans there who didn't know me from porn, they just knew this cover and came out for that. The *FHM* cover was the crossover moment of my career and really put me on the mainstream map. I ended up on their Sexiest Women in the

World list that year (number 57, not bad for a porn chick!).

That one cover brought a new level of recognition, and with that my fears and anxiety increased. I didn't feel safe doing everyday things, like shopping or getting gas, by myself. It was probably one part paranoia, one part reality. One day I was grocery shopping in my neighborhood and a guy was following me around the store. He kept his distance and didn't make contact with me, but he was definitely following me. I left that store and went to another one and he showed up there as well. That really scared me. I'd have to call Evan to rescue me sometimes be-

At the Virgin Megastore to sign copies of my FHM *cover*

cause I didn't feel safe driving home by myself and risking this guy finding out where I lived So, Evan would sometimes come out to get me or tell me to drive around a bit to make sure no one was actually following me.

The upside, of course, was that lots of new doors were opening for me. I did a ton of mainstream TV, including *E! True Hollywood Story: Rock Star Wives,* VH1's *Top 40 Hottest Rockstar Girlfriends and Wives,* WE's *The Secret Lives of Women,* A&E's *Mindfreak,* Spike TV's Guys Choice Awards, and HBO's porn documentary *Thinking XXX,* and I hosted the AVN Awards in its most pivotal year—2008, the year it finally crossed over to the mainstream by airing on Showtime for the first time.

Also in 2006 we appeared on VH1's show *SuperGroup,* which featured a bunch of musicians getting together to form a band, write a song, and play a show. Evan was invited to participate, along with such legends as Jason Bonham and Ted Nugent; one of my favorite singers ever, Sebastian Bach of Skid Row; as well as Scott Ian from Anthrax, which was the closest in genre to Evan's band, Biohazard. The show shot for about two weeks at an extravagant mansion in Las Vegas.

One week the wives were invited, and Scott's wife (and Meat Loaf's daughter), Pearl, greeted me with a big hello. I gave her an even bigger hug, and the two of us became close pals. Pearl's a very touchy-feely, huggy, warm-spirited girl, who would always greet Evan and me with a sweet kiss on the lips. We didn't think anything of it, of course, until one night Pearl was a little buzzed and said to me, "Scott doesn't want me to have sex with you."

I just thought to myself, "Hmmm. Why on Earth would she say that?" At the time I was really confused and thought, well, I guess everyone thinks that since I'm a porn star that I'm out to fuck them. Pearl and I are good friends; I respect her a lot as a woman for all she's accomplished, and not only do I think she is beautiful and talented, but she and Scott have been good friends and supporters of me.

When it came to Sebastian and his wife, Maria, though, things steamed up big-time. Sebastian and I hit it off immediately over our shared love of smoking weed. He caught me trying to roll a joint one day and laughed at my poor form. "Here, let me show you how to do that right," he said, as he took the rolling paper and some weed and rolled the perfect joint. I was a huge '80s rock fan when I was a teen and drooled over Sebastian's photos in rock magazines, so I felt like a schoolgirl every time we hung out. Sebastian was so funny about smoking. He didn't care if the VH1 cameras caught him; he only cared if Ted Nugent caught him. I think he looked up to Ted like a father figure because his own dad had passed away. He would get really paranoid of Ted finding out. (I guess now he'll know. Sorry, Sebastian.)

Sebastian's wife, Maria, was super hot, and there was a lot of innocent sexual energy between Evan and me and Sebastian and Maria. We decided to do something about all that energy. Not a foursome, though we came close! Instead, we decided to do a very sexy photo shoot of Maria and me for our husbands. It was our little treat for them. One of Evan's many talents is his photographic work, and over the years, he's photographed me many times. So he grabbed his photo equipment, even found someone to be his photo assistant, and set up a sizzling shoot in the room we were staying in. We had the best room in the house. It was a round room with hand-painted dragons on the walls, a round bed in the center, and a badass custom motorcycle for adornment . . . perfect for a photo shoot.

Sebastian was hilarious during the shoot. He kept making these noises because he was so excited to see his wife half-naked with another woman. But at the same time, he couldn't stop directing her and it seemed to make her nervous. I'll never forget when Maria laid me back on the bike and we were face to face. If it weren't for Sebastian and his big mouth interrupting the moment, who knows what would've happened. Well, *I* know what would've happened.

It wasn't all sex, drugs, and rock-and-roll during *SuperGroup*, though. Evan and I had our romantic moments too. One night, Evan told me to be ready in twenty minutes because the show's limo would be taking us somewhere. We really abused our limo privileges during that shoot. I assumed we were going to dinner or a strip club, as per usual. But instead, we pulled up to a wedding chapel, and the second I saw the chapel sign, I started to cry.

"Again?" I said to Evan, being that this would be the third time we renewed our vows.

"Yep, again," he said.

Our theory on getting married over and over again was this: You don't go to the gym just once and stay fit for life. So, why commit yourself to each other just once in your life? Renewing our vows and recommitting ourselves to each other is like maintenance for our marriage. It's constant work and needs constant reaffirmations. So, we said our "I Do's" in front of an Elvis Presley impersonator and the VH1 crew, and I felt giddy like a new bride all over again. We hopped back in the limo, closed the partition, and made love like newlyweds once again.

ONE DAY IN 2006, we got a call from the producers of Will Ferrell's movie *Blades of Glory.* His character in the movie is this washed-up ice-skating pro who is trying to make a comeback and part of his backstory was that he did a porn movie that won an AVN award called *The Iceman Cometh.* The producers were looking for two porn stars to pose with Will for a fake DVD box cover of the movie. When they called me I was thrilled and said yes immediately. They asked me who I thought should be the second girl for the shoot and I chose Stormy Daniels because we were friends and had worked together before.

Apparently, the reason they set up the shoot on a Sunday was because the producer Patrick Esposito said that people at Paramount might be uptight about having porn chicks on the lot. It was a pretty intense set. Porn shoots are so low-key, but this was very high-energy and very Hollywood. You'd hear on the walkie-talkies, "Tera and Stormy are coming out of their dressing room." "Tera and Stormy are walking." "Go for Patrick." It was so funny.

All of a sudden, we look around and there are hundreds of people looking on. Patrick told us it was 450 people to be exact, which was just about everyone who worked for or at Paramount. So much for keeping it quiet on a Sunday afternoon! The director said he'd never seen anything like this before. It was flattering.

The shoot was fun. We posed in fur bikinis with huge furry

From the Blades of Glory *shoot*

boots, looking like sexy cavewomen. When I first met Will, I was shocked at how much makeup he had on. I thought porn makeup was heavy, but it was nothing compared to movie makeup. We said our hellos to Will, and he got right down to business: "Awesome, ladies. Let's get to work." Stormy and I were on either side of Will, straddling his legs as he stood there, legs spread wide, making funny faces and cracking us up. He really has a way of contorting his face to fit the goofy character perfectly. I've never had someone make me laugh out loud without uttering a word like Will Ferrell did. He was hilarious.

"Grab Tera's hair," the director told Will, who, by the way, could not have been nicer.

Will takes a handful of my hair and picks it up like he's picking up a butterfly or something.

I told him, "No, grab it harder." I love getting my hair pulled, so I thought I'd have some fun with Will.

"I don't want to hurt you," he said.

"No, really, it's OK," I insisted.

So he grabs my hair again and it's still gentle as hell. So, Stormy gets in on the action: "Grab it, Will! Grab it harder!"

Will still wouldn't grab it harder. He kept saying, "No, no, I don't want to." Everyone's yelling, "Grab it harder!" He must have thought we were crazy. He was such a gentleman and very kind. But damn him for not yanking on my hair!

One of my favorite opportunities in 2006, though, was being on the animated show *Aqua Teen Hunger Force,* which airs on The Cartoon Network's Adult Swim. I always wanted someone to make me into a cartoon. I mean, who doesn't want to be animated, right? The funniest part is that in the show they had me in a tiny blue bikini on all fours, eating a corn dog!

When I got to the voice-over studio to tape my lines, there was a hot dog sitting on the console next to my headphones. Hmmm. That's odd, I thought. Maybe someone left their lunch in the booth. "Oh, that hot dog is for you," the director said.

"Huh?"

"Yeah, the scene calls for you to be eating a corn dog while you're talking, but we could't find one so we got you this hot dog to eat while you're reading your lines," he said.

Hmmm. Was this just a cheap ruse to get a porn star to eat a hot dog in front of them? Nope. The script really did have me chowing down. "OK. I don't eat hot dogs, but I'll give it a whirl," I said. So, down the hatch it went. I never actually watched the episode I was on until three years later, and I have to say, I cracked up over how they had me on all fours throughout the entire thing. It was hilarious. And of course, the video of me eating the hot dog made it onto YouTube and the DVD release. The episode, titled "Grim Reaper Gutters," aired on November 19, 2006.

I gained so much more recognition from all of these endeavors, which felt fantastic. But more important, I made my family proud. Sure, they had accepted my life in porn, but it wasn't exactly something they could brag about to their friends and coworkers. With the work I did in 2006 and beyond, they finally had some PG-13 things they could hold up and say, "This is my daughter!" Every time I'd get on a VH1 show or E! or in the news, they'd call up all their friends and say, "There's Linda!" Fans have asked me in the past if my family watched my work. And I just have to laugh. Yeah, right. We have Tera Patrick movie nights and eat popcorn while watching my porn. But now there are actually shows we can watch together and be proud of. It felt great that my family could finally participate in my success.

Of course, all this helped my mental state. My "crazy Tera" episodes were few and far between. I was feeling great about my career, happy, and really satisfied and rewarded for working so hard all these years. I finally got to a place where I didn't have to work as much and I could pick and choose what projects I wanted to do. And we did it our way. Evan was kicking ass as my manager, and I was happy not just for myself, but also for him. It was hard for naysayers to put him down at this point. Just three years before, I was suicidal and now we were able to have the last laugh. I'd been dragged through so much shit, and we came out smelling like roses.

Being happy in my marriage and career also helped me with my family affairs. But what especially helped was being close with Evan's family. I didn't grow up with that close-knit family unit and I've had an inconsistent relationship with my father over the years; a long-distance one with my sister Debby; and no relationship with my mother until 2009. So when the Seinfelds welcomed me with open arms, I accepted their love and let them be my family. Evan was lucky to have a mother and father still together after all these years.

I think they accepted me because they saw how in love Evan and I were and how much I cared about Evan's son, Sammy. And they respected me as a successful businesswoman. Evan says that he grew closer to his parents after we got together because it showed them that he finally was settling down in life. I learned how to be the perfect wife from Lois, Evan's mom. That was always one of my goals in life, to be a housewife in addition to a porn star. And Lois and Ira were very instrumental in bringing that side of my personality out and helping me achieve that personal goal. I learned how to cook Jewish foods, such as latkes. My favorite vacations were visiting them in Boynton Beach. I'd play shuffleboard and shop at the 99-cent store with Lois and visit museums with Ira. And they would always treat me as if I was just a normal housewife. It settled my heart.

The culmination of the year for us would be what the Seinfelds call "Fake Hanukkah." Evan's parents are "snow birds." They stay in Florida in the winter and fly up to visit the rest of the family in New York in the warmer months. So instead of celebrating Hanukkah in the dead of the December winter, we'd celebrate it on "Black Friday," the day after Thanksgiving, because it wasn't as cold and it was the latest the whole family would stay in New York. The entire family would be there, and we'd cook a huge Jewish meal with latkes, chopped liver, tongue, and corned beef. Everyone would be shouting at one another in good fun. We even had a dreidel, and would light the menorah together. It was your typical big, loud, Jewish family dinner, and I just loved it. Even though it wasn't at the year's end, it completed the year for us.

I also love being a stepmother to Sammy, who was just six years old when I met Evan. He's fifteen years old now. Sammy is such a good kid, and I took to him immediately. He called me "Twear" when we first met, and he still says that today. Between 2003 and 2008, Evan and I were bicoastal, commuting back and forth from

Los Angeles to New York to see Sammy on weekends. (Evan had partial custody—Elena had him weekdays and Evan had him weekends.) It was quite the commute for a weekend because not only did we fly for six hours cross-country, we also had to fight rush-hour Friday traffic in New York to get from our place to where Sammy lived with his mother. But I couldn't wait to do it each time.

I'd make him breakfast every morning and we'd watch *SpongeBob SquarePants* marathons when he was a kid and play video games together as he got older. I'd take him shopping at the mall, teach him how to spike his hair with gel, and just hang out and chill. When I appeared in the game *Backyard Wrestling 2: There Goes the Neighborhood* and became a special producer for *Saints Row 2,* I scored big points with him because it was something he could show off to his friends. He even got to test drive *Saints Row 2* a few months before it was released and was thrilled about that. Once he got older, we'd fly him to L.A. for weekends, and he once told us that he doesn't tell his friends about his jet-set lifestyle because they wouldn't believe him.

Tera's Tat-alogue:

I have five tattoos: a sacred heart on my ankle, an arm sleeve, a star on the inside of each wrist, and Hello Kitty on the back of my neck.

I got my first tattoo on my eighteenth birthday, in Idaho. I only had $65 to spend, so I got a small fuchsia rose on my right ankle. By 2002, it had started to fade, so I had it covered up with a sacred heart with a crown on top that says "Evan's Princess." I got that while I was on tour with Biohazard with Evan by a world-famous tattooist named Tin Tin at his

Getting my ankle done in Paris

Next to my inked version

shop in Paris. We'd only been together for two months at the time.

My next tattoos were the pink and black stars I have on the inside of my wrists. I got those done by Chris Nunez in 2006 on the TV show *Miami Ink,* and Evan got "Tera" tattooed on the side of his neck under his son's name. (Evan also has "Linda" on his wrist, and a portrait of me with devil's horns on his rib cage, by Mr. Cartoon.)

Next up was the dragon on my right arm by Hori Taku San

My Hello Kitty tattoo

at Mario Barth's Starlight Tattoo shop in the Mandalay Bay Hotel in Las Vegas. Chuck Zito and I were the first two people to get tattooed there. The outline was done with a modern tattoo gun, but the shading was done using the old-fashioned Tebori tapping style. Then Robert Atkinson finished up the arm with the cherry blossoms, water, and isobars.

And lastly, Hello Kitty is my favorite thing in the world so I just had to get a Hello Kitty tattoo. In December 2008, I got her dressed like a burlesque dancer on the back of my neck.

CHAPTER 27

So, You Want to Be a
REAL Porn Star?

When Evan and I sat down in 2003 and decided I would reenter the porn world with Teravision, I told him that I didn't want to shoot movies forever, especially not well into my thirties. Our plan was simple: Form our company, make lucrative deals, and film maybe ten movies for the next few years and then release them slowly in the coming years so there would be a steady stream of product, but I wouldn't have to shoot month after month or year after year. So when I had enough movies in the can and the mainstream media was accepting me, I figured that was the time to stop filming and focus on other things, like my lingerie line, Mistress Couture, which my sister and I launched in 2007, or the burlesque show in Las Vegas that I am launching in 2010. Or, other projects included the *Fit 4 Sex* exercise videos, the Playboy TV show *School for Sex*, the *Rock Star/Porn Star* radio show we did for Sirius Radio, and working on Teravision and my website. I didn't want to turn my back on the adult industry. I love the industry and I will forever be a part of it. I just didn't want to be fucking on camera for a living for the rest of my life.

The problem was that while I might have wanted to stop filming, Evan wasn't ready to stop. He had just begun. And he was enjoying being Spyder Jonez. He had quite a fan base and was really great on camera. So, one night in 2005 Evan sat me down and said, "Listen, you can stop doing porn. But I don't want to."

"Wait, what?" I reverted back to the jealous, insecure Tera who would scratch him up at the mere thought of him being with another girl. But I'm just like any other hot-blooded female in the world: I get jealous too. I have insecurities. I might be a porn star and head of a company, but I was also just a girl in love with a boy. And it was not easy at first to accept Evan's desires to branch out in 2005.

"Hey, you know we're doing *Test Drive* soon and I'd like to shoot a scene in it," Evan said.

"Wait, what?!" I still couldn't believe it. "You want to fuck another girl? You want to do a scene without me?"

"Well, think of this way: If I do the scene, you don't have to pay a talent fee to another guy and it saves us money," he said with a smirk.

This is when my doubts about Evan's intentions started creeping into my brain, and I started to fear that our marriage was taking a turn I didn't expect and certainly didn't want.

The only thoughts running through my mind were that he was bored of fucking me, he wanted to fuck other girls, he would find someone he liked better and leave me for her. It was irrational. Being a porn star myself I should know that it's just business. Porn stars are not like civilians. We can separate our work from our personal life. I should know, I fucked many men on-screen and it didn't affect my marriage at all. I knew this. But I was really worried nonetheless. I worked my whole life to get to this place where I had my prince charming, and I didn't want to lose that. That scared the hell out of me. I was afraid he'd find a saner girl and finally say to me, "You know what, Tera? You're crazy. I can't take it." I just kept thinking, "But why?" No matter what reason he gave me, I would say, "But why?" There was no right answer.

We were both working so hard when it came to Teravision. He had put his music career on hold to be my CEO. And he wasn't done living out his porn fantasies on-screen. He wanted to get his freak on, and that had nothing to do with his feelings toward me. You see, the difference between me and Evan is that Evan is ten times hornier than I am.

My big point was this: almost every couple in porn breaks up, and I didn't want to be another porn statistic. I didn't want the porn curse to hit us. I've seen it happen to other couples. Doing porn as a husband and wife team is safe, but once one branches out to do people outside the marriage, that's when the trouble seems to set in, and I feared for our perfect marriage.

After the initial shock wore off, I was able to think rationally about the situation. I would be a hypocrite to not let him do other women for movies. I was doing other men and it didn't hurt our marriage one bit. It's just fucking, and with all the crew and cameras around, it's more of a job than an intimate situation. We're all professionals. You shake hands with your costar, you do your job, and you leave. There's no attachment. If I wasn't in porn and Evan wasn't doing a scene, would I have let him fuck another girl? No. But we *are* in porn and it *was* for a scene, so the answer had to be yes.

And besides, I knew Evan loved me, and that is all that mattered. I knew I was his princess. I knew I had his heart. He reminded me of it morning, noon, and night from the time we met. Our marriage was solid. We weren't like other porn couples. I finally calmed down and realized that I could let him do this and it would be OK.

"OK, you can do the scene," I finally said. "Let's see how it goes and how I feel afterwards."

"Thank you, baby," Evan said. "You'll see. When I come home from the set, I will still be your loving husband, and nothing will have changed."

"OK," I said. "But one thing—I don't want to be on set when you do your scenes. I don't want to see it. I don't want to hear about it." He promised me he'd do it only for a few years and then get out. Fair enough.

I trusted him, and off he went to do his first scene without me. It was a normal boy-girl sex scene with Roxy Jezel. And Evan was right. He came home from set that day and nothing had changed. We went to bed that night in each other's arms as if nothing had happened that day and as if nobody else in the world mattered but us.

I had a few conditions, of course. Absolutely under no circumstances could he do anal with another girl. That was our thing, and I wanted to keep it that way. There was another condition that I had to attach later. Once Evan launched his own pay website Rock starpimp.com in 2008, he started doing scenes with girls every week. I never wanted to get involved with it, but one day I asked him, "So, what do you do with the girls?" He said, "Well, you know, I ask their name. I interview them. I spin them around. And then we have sex."

"You WHAT?!" I screamed. "You spin them?!"

Spinning does have another meaning: a spinner in porn is a petite girl a guy spins on his dick. But that's not the spinning we're talking about here. *That* spinning would be OK. The spinning that I had a temper tantrum over meant that he would take the girl by her hand and twirl her around to get a good look . . . like a dancer does to his partner or a daddy does to his little girl or as Evan did to me on our first date and many dates thereafter. From our very first date, Evan would love to see me get all dressed up for a night out on the town and when I was ready, he'd take me by the hand, spin me around, and give me a kiss. And now he was doing our special thing with these porn chicks?! Oh, no. Not on my watch.

"That's *our* cutesy little thing!" I screamed at Evan.

"Uh . . ." He was speechless.

I continued my tirade. "You're doing our special thing with those girls?!"

"I'm sorry. I didn't think—" Evan said.

"That's right, you didn't think!" I just welled up inside and the floodgates of tears opened up and I cried and cried and cried.

"I'm sorry. I'll never do that again. I should've known," he said. He felt truly awful. He apologized profusely and did everything to make it up to me. He came home one day soon after that and pulled into the driveway holding two huge bunches of red roses out the window as he drove in. My heart melted. He also got in the habit of buying me expensive gifts or sending me shopping on the days he had scenes to take my mind off what he was doing on set.

Here is the column I wrote on the topic of couples in the business in my "Teravision" column for *Genesis* magazine in February 2009:

So many people ask me about what it is like to be in porn and to be married. I mean is that really that far-fetched? What is it like to work in an office and come home to a spouse that is tired and stressed out and not interested in fucking? So many married people I know are living in complete lies pretending for their partner that they don't want to enjoy sex with other people. Our society is built on this puritanical concept of monogamy when to me, we are all beautiful sexual creatures who were meant to enjoy sex to the fullest. I don't know if this constant test of denial and restraint is what was meant for human beings.

For a lot of women in the business, I think there is a lot of fear as I had before I met my husband, as to "Who is ever going to love me?" or "Who is not going to judge me?" There is still a stigma attached for a lot of men who are very intimidated by women who are sexually free, sexually open, or especially porn stars. Obviously, for some couples, it is easier if they are both in the business, because there is a level of understanding about what goes on in the industry. Sometimes it works better in certain couples' dynamics when one partner is in the business and the other is a civilian. Very often one partner can become very jealous and this can be extremely problematic. Especially when you think that confidence is probably the single sexiest trait someone can have to me, and jealousy the single biggest turnoff. The adult film business is obviously a breeding ground for unhealthy relationships. I feel very fortunate to have been able to have a healthy marriage within the industry.

The adult business provides a great boundary and actual safe haven for some couples who want to live out their fantasies. My husband and I both get to have sex with whoever we want on camera, but in our personal lives we are more of a "traditional" couple. For Evan and I, who have really open and honest communication, this really works for us as we both get to have the best of both worlds. I live out all my fantasies and still have the security of having a caring and devoted partner.

Additionally, to get over that initial fear that your partner will cheat on you, introducing sex with other people can actually be the most freeing thing in the world. The first time your partner has sex with someone else, and comes home to you, you realize that person is with you because it is a conscious decision and a choice rather than something they feel trapped by. If it wasn't so taboo, it would not be a great topic of intriguing discussion. Bottom line is that fucking and sucking feels great and drives that intangible sixth sense of ours, but love makes the world go round!

Although every couple has their own rules, it is nice to see other couples in the industry who have positive successful relationships. I just adore Gina Lynn and Travis Knight. They are a smoking hot couple who are very much in love, but also both work in the adult industry. I have known them for many years and they, like my husband and I, seem to have a stronger relationship than

many civilian couples. Evan Stone and Syren, Jules Jordan and
Jenna Haze, Nicole Sheridan and Voodoo, Jessica Drake and Brad
Armstrong, the list goes on and on. So bottom line, porn stars
need love too and sex is the reason you are reading *Genesis*. So
whenever possible have your cake and eat it too!

CHAPTER 28

Mission Accomplished

Hall of Fame? Really? I don't know how I feel about that," I told Evan when he informed me that I was going to be inducted into the AVN Hall of Fame on January 10, 2009. "Does that make me old?"

"No, it's an honor, honey," he assured me. "Look at how much you've accomplished. Most girls in the industry last a few years. You've been at the top for ten."

After I got over the shock that I was a ten-year vet, I realized I do have a lot to be proud of. I've accomplished my goals, learned a lot, and have a lot to show for it. To me, the induction marked the beginning of a new chapter in my life rather than the ending of an old one. And it means I can pick and choose what I work on more selectively.

I am now able to focus on things I can only do *because* of my time in front of the camera, such as working on my lingerie line, modeling, hosting parties around the world as an ambassador of all things sexy, and working on my upcoming burlesque show in Las Vegas that I plan to debut later in 2010. My love for the adult industry runs deep. I am grateful to my fans for raising me up on this pedestal, and I hope they will follow me wherever this road takes me.

Being inducted into the Hall of Fame felt like closure on one part of my porn life. I did what I wanted to do and I accomplished my goals. And it cemented me in the industry forever, for which I will always be proud and grateful. Grateful because if it weren't for porn, I might not have met the man of my dreams and I wouldn't be able to live my life the way I want to now.

This particular AVN was also extra special not only because it celebrated a decade of my life, but it was also the fifth anniversary of my wedding, which meant even more to me than my work accomplishments. I accomplished a happy life. After seven years (five married) of crazy ups and downs, I had a man who still wanted to marry me over and over again like he promised on our wedding night in 2004. So on our fifth wedding anniversary, the night before my Hall of Fame induction, Evan surprised me again for a fourth time with yet another renewal of our vows. Yes, Elvis was there once again. Yes, it once again felt like the first time. But what was different this time was that I finally felt true peace. As I walked down that aisle of our hotel suite, which he'd sprinkled with pink rose petals and lined with candles, and I looked up at Evan standing there, everything felt perfectly right with my world . . . except for one thing: my relationship with my mother.

Having grown close to Evan's family over the years made me think about my own relations. My dad and I were always fine. The thing with Dad is this: He's not malicious. He's not a bad guy. He hasn't done anything horrible. He's just this carefree individual who would come and go a lot. I'd go months without talking to him, but it wasn't because anything bad happened. It's just the way it was. I know he loves me and is proud of me, and that's what matters.

Now, my mother is another story. I didn't talk to her for seventeen years. She had written me a letter when I was sixteen that I didn't open and read until I sat down to write this book. I was afraid of what the letter would say. It was right around the time I came home from Japan and I knew she disapproved of what my lifestyle was like there: sex, drugs, and rock-and-roll.

But there was nothing to fear. She wrote, "Dear, Linda, I just want you to know that I really missed you. I missed your beautiful face around me. I still love you a lot no matter what." Once I read that, nothing else mattered. I realized it was time to let go of the past and let my mother back into my life. My sister Debby was trying to get my mother and me back together, but she hadn't been talking to my dad that much, so I told her that I'd call Mom if she'd call Dad. And that's just what we did.

It's so nice having my mom in my life now. All of the anger and hurt feelings are gone, and we are able to rebuild a healthy mother-daughter relationship. She's even living with me now in my second home in Las Vegas, which we got in 2009 so I'd have a place to

With my sister Debby

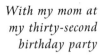

*With my mom at
my thirty-second
birthday party*

stay in town when I host my monthly party at TAO, an Asian nightclub in the Venetian Resort Hotel Casino.

It's weird how we could be apart for most of our lives but still
have so much in common. We do weird things the same way, things
that no one else does. There will be times where we take the words
out of the other's mouth. I wash my feet in the sink like she does.
I use a mortar and pestle to crush herbs when I cook on the floor
like she does. It's so odd.

My mom says of me, "I missed her. It feels like just yesterday, like
nothing happened. We picked up where we left off, but better. I'm
just happy that she is happy and good. And I'm happy we reconnected. I see the American Dream in her."

Mom and I plan to go to Thailand together soon to connect with
our culture and visit our relatives. She says I didn't get my temper
from her. I got it from *her* mother, my grandmother, whom I've never
met. We'll see. I never thought I'd get to this place in life: love, success, mental sanity, and family. I feel like I finally have it all.

You Asked, I Answered:

12 BURNING QUESTIONS FROM MY FANS

1. *What was the scariest thing that happened on a shoot?*

—BRIAN, 27, LOS ANGELES

In 2001, I was at a shoot for someone else's movie at Digital Playground at a Muslim's house in Paris, France. I don't remember what the shoot was for, but I was just there to hang out and have Ali take some photos of me. The owner of the house was really happy to have a porn shoot going on right before his eyes. He was really into it. But apparently he didn't tell his wife what he was up to. All of a sudden, the wife storms into the house, screaming at her husband and at all of us in French like a crazy person. She rushed into the kitchen and grabbed a knife and literally chased me out of the house with the knife in her hand. I grabbed the keys to our rented passenger van and bolted for the door as Ali and the others scrambled to collect their equipment. I was so flustered that as soon as I started the van to leave, I crashed it into the wall. Luckily, it was still drivable and we peeled out of there as fast as we could, laughing all the way.

2. *What is the most embarrassing moment of your career?*

—LISA, 24, SAN DIEGO

When my vagina got molded for a toy called the Tera Patrick Fleshlight, which is a custom mold of my pussy. It's the number-one bestselling male sex toy. I was leaning back, and plaster was over the whole area—from my clit to my asshole—and I totally farted and there was this giant hole in the mold, so I had to do

259

it over again. We couldn't release a toy with a giant fart-bubble in it!

3. *Do you watch your own porn, and is that weird?*

—JAMES, 32, CHICAGO

No. This may be surprising, but I don't watch my own movies. I don't even have copies of all of my videos. I subscribe to this theory that once I do it, it's over for me. I don't save them. I don't watch them. I lived the fantasy. It was done. And I don't need to see it again. I've never even watched any of my movies. Never.

4. *What's your favorite celebrity encounter?*

—KELLY, 36, FORT LAUDERDALE

Actually, Kanye West was really nervous when he met me backstage at Fashion Week in L.A. in 2007. He told Evan, "Dude, I have the biggest favor to ask you. I really want to meet Tera, but I'm really shy. I don't know what to say to her." It was really sweet, though. I'm always flattered when other celebrities come up to me to say hi, or even ask for an autograph or to take a photo of me. It's weird to think that Kanye West has seen my pussy, but I can't see his dick. In a way, that's not fair. Ha!

5. *Is it weird to think that people you know and people you meet have seen your porn and masturbate to you?*

—MIKE, 23, VAN NUYS

Yeah, it's a little weird to know that someone talking to me has seen my innermost parts and I haven't seen theirs. But it's not weird that they masturbate to me. They also masturbate to Cameron Diaz and Carmen Electra and Jessica Alba and the girl at the grocery store. Men are just visual. I'm no different, except they have a little bit more to masturbate to, they see a little bit more of me. It's just humbling.

6. *What advice do you have for new girls getting into the industry?*

—LEISHA, 21, NEWARK

Make sure you are making the decision with a clear head and that nobody else is influencing you. At the end of the day, you have to live with what you've done and remember that your third-grade teacher may see you one day, your father may see you, any kids you have, your nieces and nephews—everybody. So look your best and know this is out there for everyone to see and you can't take it back. And don't party or get caught up in the party scene. This business attracts the bad boyfriend, the suitcase pimp who comes into the business and latches onto a porn girl or a model. It's hard to find a good guy in this industry. And just know that you really can make a lot of money, so invest it wisely. Don't buy the newest Balenciaga bag. Invest in real estate instead.

7. *What's the most embarrassing thing that happened to you in high school?*

—ROWYAN, 29, IRELAND

I blossomed early and had 34Cs by the time I was thirteen. So in high school one day when we were changing for swim class, a few of my classmates were teasing me for my big breasts, saying they were like balloons, and they started saying, "Let's lay her down and pop her!" I was very insecure at the time.

8. *Why don't you speak Thai?*

—LISA, 38, VANCOUVER, CANADA

I get this from my fans a lot. My mom never taught us how to speak her language. My mom, Preeya, explains, "I wanted the best for her. We lived in California for so many years and it was English or Spanish, no Thai. So I never taught her Thai. When I sent her to school, I just wanted her to know English. No one spoke Thai, so we didn't teach our girls that. I didn't think it would be useful. She knew the colors and numbers in Thai, though." I still know those today. But that's all I know. Mom and I are going to go to Thailand sometime soon. Now that I'm older and have reconnected with my mom, I want to embrace my Thai heritage more.

9. *What is the best pickup line anyone has used on you?*

—JESSICA, 24, TOLEDO

I love cheesy pickup lines. My favorite line is this: "You know what would look good on you? Me!" I'm easy, haven't you figured it out yet? Besides, do you really need a pickup line to pick up a porn star?

10. *What Teravision movie are you most proud of and why?*

—JENNIFER, 22, NEW YORK

I'm truly proud of them all. But one that stands out from a production standpoint is *InTERActive*, an interactive movie from the point of view of the male user, which we shot in 2006 with Hustler Video. It took the format to a new level by putting a storyline around it and using real cum shots. Evan and I are big fans of sexy storylines, so for this one we hired a Robert De Niro look-alike and I played his lonely, bored housewife having an affair on him. And most movies in this format use fake cum shots, which is a cheat. I'm proud that *InTERActive* used all real cum shots and they were all by the talented Spyder Jonez. This movie is one of my bestselling DVDs and has the best recurring sales of any of my movies. And it won the Best Interactive DVD Award at the 2008 AVN Awards and set the record as the fastest-selling *Hustler* release.

11. *Weren't you afraid of catching an STD? How come in some movies you use condoms and in others you don't?*

—LEXI, 19, MIAMI

I never worried about contracting an STD because, for one, when I started out in 1999, there were a smaller number of guys working, so everyone either knew them or knew of them and word spreads fast if something's not right. But I always required that the guys I worked with not only take the obligatory HIV test, but get the full panel STD test, which includes chlamydia, gonorrhea, syphilis, and others. And I can honestly say that I think it's safer to have sex with someone in the porn industry as opposed to picking up a guy or chick at a club. The porn guy can hand you a paper that shows his test results. The club guy can't. That said, I still do feel very lucky that I never caught anything. As for condoms, some companies require that you work with a condom, others don't. If they don't require it, you still have a choice to have the guy wear one. If a guy had the full STD test, I was fine with him not wearing a condom.

12. *Do you ever keep going even after the director says cut?*

—MEAGAN, 24, SEATTLE

Sure! When you're really into it, it's hard to stop. One of my favorite female performers to work with was Briana Banks, whom I did *Collision Course* with. I was really into working with her, because I knew she was nuts—she was just really into sex and loved women and she's done everything—a lot more than I've done. I had a feeling she was going to try to "outfuck" me, so as a preemptive strike, I grabbed her first and laid her down to eat her out. I just went for it. I was licking her pussy and I was really turned on, so when the director, Skeeter Kerkove, said cut, I just kept on going. And I made her cum!

My Sexy Tips for Guys and Gals:

For the guys . . .

TRIM THE TRUNK: This means no trouser forest, no bad breath, and no body odor. Shave, trim, shave, trim, brush, and shave again. Although I like my men rough and rugged, this doesn't mean stinky, sweaty, or hairy! Invest in a good trimmer (Andis is a great brand) and shave with the Gillette Fusion (five blades). No beating around the bush, boys. Shave those balls until they are silky smooth. I personally love balls in my mouth when they are hairless. You can neatly trim the rest of the hair above your member without going full porno shave, but if this is your first time trimming the hedges, you will notice that your cock looks bigger the more you trim, and who doesn't love that?

SMELL DELICIOUS: Scent is such a powerful aphrodisiac and it's not relied upon enough. When sexy cologne is mixed with your natural pheromones, your girl is bound to get even more turned on. You don't need to buy expensive fancy cologne, but putting in a little effort for her senses will really show you care. I like old-school manly-man scents such as Old Spice, Drakkar Noir, and Fahrenheit. Newer colognes that rock my world, though, are Prada, Serge Lutens, and Gucci Rush.

DIRTY MOUTH? CLEAN IT!: I know I don't need to remind you guys of this, but brush those teeth regularly, use mouthwash, and *always* carry Listerine pocket strips. You never know when you might hook up. Don't chew gum, because it might tire out your mouth, and you need to save energy for marathon pussy-eating.

EAT OUT: Pussy eating, cunnilingus, going down, dining at the Y . . . call it whatever you want, but make sure you pay extra attention to the details down there. The clitoris is the woman's pleasure button, so press it, lick it, flick it, nibble it, tease it, bite it (gently), rub it, blow on it, tickle it, suck it, and spell the alphabet on it with your tongue and look for her reaction. When you hear her moan, she is telling you that you are doing something right. So do it some more. Fingers are a great accompaniment to eating pussy, but sometimes less is more. Tease her and make her want it. Don't go deep or hard until she begs you. Do *not* treat a girl's nether regions like they are beef jerky. Do follow her lead, ask her what she likes and what she wants. We don't expect you to know everything, but you should know the basics.

TOY WITH ME: Sexually liberated women of the millennium have their stash of dildos, pocket rockets, and even porn. However, it is such a turn-on when you guys acknowledge our need to explore and bring us home a surprise. Candy and flowers are still good. Champagne and diamonds, even better. But bringing home a good sex toy like a pair of fur-lined handcuffs, warming lube, a powerful vibrator, or a big fat dildo can totally energize a woman for marathon sex sessions. Advanced toys to buy: Anal love beads and graduated butt plugs can take you to new heights, but don't forget the lube (Eros brand lube is my fave).

SPLURGE ONCE IN A WHILE: Girls love to be spoiled. A spoiled girl is a turned-on girl, and a turned-on girl likes to put out for her man. If you're not sure what to get your lady, I have three suggestions for some high-end goodies: sexy lingerie (try my own brand, Mistress Couture, but Agent Provocateur rocks too), high heels (try Giuseppe Zanotti or Christian Louboutin on for size), and a glamorous dress (Dolce & Gabbana or Herve Leger are two of my faves). If your lady *feels* sexy, she will *be* sexy, and that's a win-win for both of you.

GET ADVENTUROUS: The best way to spice up your sex life is to be open to new adventures. Try having sex in spontaneous places—fuck her in your car, fuck her in the dressing room at the mall, fuck her in the fancy hotel room you surprised her with, fuck her any place she hasn't been fucked before. And don't forget to take her to sexually charged environments like swingers' clubs, strip clubs, or fetish bars.

FOR THE GALS . . .

TAKE CONTROL: When it comes to sex, the woman usually holds all the cards and has the power to give sex the green light. You've got the pussy power. We decide if, when, where, and how it is going to go down. So use that power wisely. Tell your man exactly what you want. Men are not mind readers, but the good ones take direction well. Let them know when you are wet and horny. Make them pull that car over to fuck you then and there.

DRESS TO IMPRESS: Whether it's a first date or someone you are shacked up with, you should always dress to impress. Invest in good lingerie that fits well. (Stay away from "one size fits all." It doesn't.) Try Agent Provocateur, and of course, my very own private label, Mistress Couture. If you look sexy, you feel sexy and if you feel sexy, well then you are sexy! Trust me, knowing you have crotchless panties on under your business suit or jeans will put a little extra pep in your step. Also, heels not only add a few inches, but they also lift your booty, improve your posture, and lengthen your legs. So, leave the shoes on, ladies, especially when you are going to do some standing doggy!

GET CREATIVE: As much as many men love their partner to be nothing more than a fuck doll who gets tossed around, it is good to have a few tricks up your sleeve. Go back and reread the section on page 66 on sexual positions or watch my porn to get some visual tips and tricks. For example, reverse cowgirl in front of a mirror not only gives you G-spot stimulation, but gives your man a full view of your beautiful body. You may not want to try compromising positions like a pile driver on your first date.

KITTY GROOMING: A well-groomed kitty is a happy kitty. Whether you want to go bald with a full Brazilian wax job or leave a California landing strip, a nice presentation of your private parts is important. The pros prefer to wax, and I personally get waxed monthly at the Honey Suite in Sherman Oaks, California, where the lovely Dana cares for my kitty. Before an on-camera sex scene, it is common courtesy for the girl to douche before being intimate. The same should go for off-camera sex. It keeps you feeling fresh and smelling good and will encourage your man or woman to go down on you all night long. Another trick of the trade: always use an enema before anal sex. It will provide you the confidence to really let go.

GO FOR IT: Overcome your sexual inhibitions. Be a flirt, watch porn, have a threesome, try anal sex, or have a one-night stand. Experiment with public sex, give good phone sex, do a girl, kiss strangers. . . . Whatever you do, just be safe and be sexy! It is the only life you have, so go out and live it to the fullest. Tell 'em Tera said so!

AFTERWARD...

"SLEEPING BEAUTY WAKES UP"

10/12/09

Well, I never thought I'd be writing this chapter. Over the course of putting together this book over the past year, a lot has changed. And the biggest change is that I am no longer with Evan. You probably already know this, as I announced I was divorcing him in September. Oh boy, did our haters have a field day with that news. But it's OK. When my writer, Carrie, and my editor asked me if I wanted to rewrite the book in light of this postdeadline development, I told them no. I meant everything I said and my feelings, thoughts, and ideals were all real at the time. I meant every word of it and I have no regrets. Even though one decision I made early on—the one to let him get into porn—is what ultimately ended my relationship with Evan, I don't even regret that decision. Let me explain.

Evan and I have been through a lot together. He got me through my suicide attempt, my mental craziness, and my painful split from Digital Playground. He also took me to new heights and helped me achieve more than I ever thought I would. He helped me reap the financial rewards that I couldn't achieve with Digital. Through those experiences, he taught me strength and helped bring out the

Tera in me who is smarter, wiser, and more independent. Even though now Evan and I are on separate paths and need to follow our different dreams, I will forever be grateful to him for bringing out the strong woman I always knew I had in me. I wish him the best in the next phase of his life. Life is a journey and Evan has been the most important step in my journey so far. But as I grew with him, I got to a point in life where I learned to be more secure, and I realized I could do it on my own. Writing this book, too, was a journey of self-discovery, an awakening. I see things differently now and my priorities have changed.

Though Evan and I grew together over our seven-year relationship, we have also grown apart over the past year. We each want different things. I learned that I want to have a normal life. I want a traditional marriage and I want to be a mom. Porn is my past. Evan wants to finish what he started in porn. If you want the dirt, here it is. I gave him an ultimatum: Give up your porn career or give up me. He wouldn't give up porn. Of course, I was heartbroken at first, but now I feel free. Free to do what I really want to do. Free to live my life in a different way. Free to get the happy ending I always wanted, which was to marry a rock star, live happily ever after, and have it be just about me and him. Not him, me, and whatever chick he's fucking the next day. What was once OK to me is no longer OK.

To explain how it went down, I'll have to start by explaining my choice in men. As you might have noticed while reading this book, I've always been attracted to the bad boy, the rocker, the biker, and the rebel. But with that comes the good and the bad. I don't want to blame my father, but I would not be honest if I didn't admit that maybe his not always being in my life is what drove me to domineering, alpha males. I've depended too much on the men in my life and given them an opening to take control. Over the years, I've let men have power over me. It's a pattern I now see. Good or bad, love him or hate him, Evan is a domineering alpha male.

I think my dad knows his absence has affected my relationships, and I think he feels a little guilty about that and knows that is why I gravitate to men who are controlling. I love my dad, but by the same token, when I've needed my dad at certain times in my life, he hasn't been there. Other boyfriends have been there and Evan was really there for me. Evan helped me through a lot and helped me be more independent and secure. So independent and secure, in fact, that I was able to walk away from him when I decided things weren't right. But don't get me wrong. I'm not blaming Daddy. I did this all on my own, and that's OK. That's what growing up is all about.

When I started my courtship with Evan, he was a rock star and acting on one of the hottest shows on TV, HBO's *Oz*. I wanted to marry a rock star and live happily ever after. I didn't want to marry a porn star, and that is what he became. I thought I had my dream fulfilled, but ultimately the dream backfired on me. I know Evan loved me and still does, but I also see that I was his way into porn. (OK, haters, this is where you scream, "No shit!" Go ahead and say it or think it. I can take it. My eyes are wide open now.) He was looking for his entry into porn and he got it through me. So, yeah, I do feel used to some extent, but I can't discount what he did for me in the process. People will gossip and say, "You're just seeing this now?!" But my answer to that is this: I was blinded by love. I believed he would only do porn for a few years and move on. I truly believed him.

Evan achieved his goal, but in the end I suffered. He was the dominating male who ran my life, and in that I lost a lot of myself. He was living the dream—he was going to bed with Tera Patrick at night and going to work in the morning and fucking another girl. I wanted a husband for life who only loved and wanted me. I wasn't living my dream. However, in the moment, I thought I was.

On days he would shoot, he'd buy me an expensive gift like Christian Louboutin shoes or Agent Provocateur lingerie, or send me shopping. I might have mistaken those tokens as love then, but I don't buy it now. At the time, I was accepting of it because I knew he loved me and cared about me and would come home to me. He'd come back from a shoot with flowers and act all lovey-dovey, and it was fine for a while. I thought I was OK, but as time went on, I realized material things like Gucci bags and a closet full of clothes and a nice car and a beautiful house (like that Talking Heads' song "Once in a Lifetime") wasn't what I wanted. Like the song, I questioned, "How did I get here?"

I wanted to marry a rock star, live happily ever after, get out of porn, and get into mainstream. But Evan loves being in porn. That's his dream now. My love wasn't enough to keep us together. His take was this: "I'm having a great time. I'm having my cake and I get to eat it, too." But all I could think toward the end was "What about my cake?" I was willing to let him get into porn to make him happy, but I was sacrificing my own happiness, though I didn't know it at the time. He wouldn't make that one sacrifice for me.

The beginning of the end for us was at the 2009 AVN Awards in January in Las Vegas when I was inducted into the AVN Hall of Fame to commemorate my ten years in the business—five years on my own and five years with Evan. After getting off that stage at AVN, I said, "I'm done." I had accomplished what I set out to do. What else can I do in adult film? I did it all. I conquered a man's world. I was the only woman other than Jenna Jameson who had started her own company and moved on to hire girls and make beautiful movies. I had worked very hard for a very long time and had accomplished what I set out to do. It was time for phase two of my life, but I didn't know it just yet.

From January 2009 until my thirty-third birthday on July 25, 2009, which was when we were in the middle-to-late stages of writing this book, I began to really reevaluate my life, my goals, my true needs, and think about what my future held. I thought a lot about Evan—the good and the bad. This wasn't a rash decision. I searched my heart and soul for those seven months, but on my birthday, my decision was etched in stone.

At my party at the Tao nightclub in Las Vegas, there was a pivotal moment when I looked up at Evan, and when he looked back, his eyes did not say, "This is my wife and I adore her and I'm so proud of her and I'm happy to be here with her on her birthday." His eyes said, "Yeah, whatever." I felt like a trophy wife. I felt like this shiny polished AVN award that he was picking up when it was convenient, putting in the spotlight, fanning and waving, and putting it back on the shelf when he was done. Then he would go to party with Cuba Gooding Jr. or Brett Ratner, which is exactly what he did that night. Evan spent more time with Cuba at my birthday party then he did with me, his fucking wife, at my own birthday party. I felt taken for granted and I felt used. I didn't want to be there. I was in a crowded club where all my fans looked at me with more love, devotion, and admiration than my own husband did.

Evan got what he wanted. He got the trophy wife. He got the big house and the nice cars. He got into porn. He got his connections. He got into the hottest clubs in Vegas, Miami, Los Angeles, and around the world. He regained the fame he once lost from no longer being on *Oz* or in a hot band. But I didn't get my dream: a man to love me, be with me, change with me, and evolve with me. The look of true love in his eyes was gone.

And I remember feeling that emptiness in Tao. All of a sudden I sat down and the music was pulsating and everyone was crowding around me—that was the life-changing moment for me. That switch in my head went off; I got that feeling in my stomach I used to get telling me something is not right here. I felt awful. I didn't feel like a wife or a person. Early on it wasn't about parading me around town; it was about our love, him and I, and that changed. That was really painful. It's painful to be writing these words. I never thought this would happen. I never thought we'd be in *this* place.

During those seven months between AVN and my birthday, I felt like I was living in a cloud. My thinking slowly evolved during that time. I was technically living the dream, but what was once fulfilling became unfulfilling. That birthday was reflective for me. Birthdays are always like that for me. Evan always made my special day into *his* special day—a big party at a flashy club that was very showy with lots of presents, celebrity guests, and people I didn't know. I once liked that, but I no longer do. My next birthday will be at my house with my family and a few close friends who truly care and love *me*, not "Tera Patrick, the porn star," and who won't be looking over my shoulder to see if a more interesting celebrity or connection is walking in.

I gave him an ultimatum. I did. I don't care if that sounds bad; it's what I had to do. I said to Evan, "I'm your wife and that is the strongest bond two people should have, and that should come first. I've moved on from porn. And I want you to stop. You promised me you'd only do porn for a few years. Your few years are up. It's your porn career or me."

(I haven't shot a movie since 2006, when we put a ton of footage in the can. If you see a DVD dated 2007, 2008, or 2009, it was shot around 2006. The only porn I've done recently was a sex scene I did with Evan for his website in 2009, which was just my way of showing my undying love and support for him.)

"Listen," I told him, early one morning in our Sherman Oaks house, "I love you. We've achieved so much. Look at what we've done. I will always love you. But I just want to put the marriage first. You know I'm not doing porn anymore. I've written this book as closure to that chapter of my life, and I've been inducted into the Hall of Fame, cementing ten years in this business, which is a good point to stop. I'm doing my Vegas burlesque show. I'm getting offers for reality shows. Life has gone on for me. I'm on to phase two of my life and career now. I'm done with phase one. I'm not turning my back on it. I'll keep terapatrick.com and I want us to keep our baby, Teravision, alive. But you're my husband. You are a rock star. I want you to pursue your music career instead of a porn career. You pursue music and mainstream acting, and I'll pursue my new ventures."

And he said, in typical Evan fashion, "Don't give an ultimatum. No one will ever give me an ultimatum. I'm not going to quit. Why would I want to quit?"

I was surprised at his response. I truly thought the power of love would make him see the light. I would've done anything to keep him, but eventually I had to do what was right for me.

His goal was to become a porn star, and he got it. I realized I didn't come first to him anymore, and that broke my heart. It was the hardest thing I've had to face. I took my Hello Kitty suitcase and my dogs Chopper and Mr. Big Time, packed them in the pink smart car Evan had given me on Valentine's Day, and headed off. As I drove off, I started thinking, "OMG, my whole life sits in a safe in my Sherman Oaks home—all of my finances, my business papers, my security—and it is with him. I need my own safe. My own financial independence."

"Where are you going?!" he screamed, running out the door and waving me down. And I said, "I'm going to be with my mother in Vegas." He didn't believe that I could drive those 280 miles to Las Vegas by myself because I had never done it before, but I did it. It felt like a *Thelma and Louise* moment (just without the tragic ending). I cranked up Madonna's "Jump" and Linkin Park's "In the End" and drove and cried the whole way to Vegas, never looking back. And that is when I felt truly empowered and free. For once I was not afraid to be alone. I knew I could do this. Hell, it was Evan who had helped me get strong. I made up my mind and stuck to it and soon filed for divorce. As fate would have it, I filed for divorce on September 4, 2009, which was the seventh anniversary of our first official date. Though it was my choice, that doesn't mean I wasn't devastated. I so wanted him to tell me he would quit and put me first. I so wanted him to tell me he loved me and would do anything for me. But he didn't and that will forever hurt.

My mom and sister really got me through this. You don't love a man for seven years and not have doubts. I reflected on our life together over tears with Mom and Sis in my Vegas house for weeks. I truly thought we had the game plan down and I was the luckiest girl in the world. I thought past through the days I tried to kill myself, through the dark days of Digital Playground. I remembered all of that and in my heart I remember feeling he was the only one who would hold me, the only one who would love me, and now all I could think about was "How did it get to this?" That's what I agonized over. I knew it was over, but I thought, "How did I get here? How did this happen? Why can't love keep people together? Why wasn't my love enough to keep him with me? Why was porn so much more important to him than me?

Finally, I would wake up in my bed in Vegas every morning, look to my mom and say, "Mom, I'm happy to be here. This is where I truly belong: in Vegas with you, starting a new chapter in my life." I never looked back. I realized I had been slowly falling out of love with him this past year and lost all respect for him. That said, I woke up for many mornings during this transitional time feeling a little unsure of my future, but the one thing I was 100 percent sure of was that I was making the right decision.

My mom said to me, "If you want to go back to him, I won't judge you. Whatever you want to do, I'm here for you. You may take him back ten more times. You may go through this for six more months. Hell, you may be back with him by the time this book is out. But just know that you can do this. You can live on your own. The days of making sacrifices are over for you. And he woke that up in you. He took you on a wonderful journey and now you're on another journey."

She was a strong base of support and nonjudgmental guidance, and that's what I needed. I didn't want to hear "He's an asshole.

You should've done this a long time ago." I'm sure lots of people thought that, but it's not helpful or fair to our marriage or to Evan, and it disrespects me. I can't and won't dismiss what we had.

My sister Debra was by my side too. She's my new assistant and is helping me with my new ventures. Ever since Debra and I were little girls, she has taken care of me. She is the caretaker, and that's how she helped me get through this part of my life. When we were young and I was going through a tough time, she knew exactly how to cheer me up: grilled cheese sandwiches. Debra's are the best. We ate a lot of grilled cheese sandwiches during this time. Debra has been my rock throughout my life and the one constant family member who has been there for me.

I think the most liberating feeling I've had day-to-day is waking up in my house in Las Vegas, being in a whole new city, and thinking, "Wow, I own everything in this house. I worked for this. This is all mine. It's not his and mine. It's mine." I love that I'm on my own now. It's such a liberating feeling. I'm so much happier. Not to say there hasn't been pain or that I wasn't happy before. I was happy. You don't stay with someone for seven years without there being true happiness. There's so much passion between us—both in love and in hate. And don't think for a second that our on-screen passion wasn't real. It was. Evan was my favorite performer to work with. On a day-to-day basis, do I think of him? Of course I do. I think of him, but not in the same way as before. I guess I was going through this for a long time. I was slowly waking up every day thinking, "Hmmm, what's going on? What's happening?" And I finally figured it out.

As I said, writing the book really empowered me. It made me reevaluate my life and reprioritize my needs. It was a turning point and a process of self-discovery for me. And it was a process of regaining control because I'd been out of control for so long. My split from Evan kind of reminds me of my split from my old manager at Digital Playground, Samantha. We can't discuss the details of the divorce, as I couldn't discuss the details of the split from Digital, but I can say I've had to make some financial sacrifices—I'm stronger now and can handle it. And, besides, Evan did earn it. We didn't have a prenuptial agreement when we married, but I'm not getting screwed. And, oddly, I really don't wish him any ill will.

I have my family back. I have my sister. I have my mother—a real support system for once. And equally as important, I have my sense of self and my wits about me and now I know too much. I have my pride and I'm OK. It was like Sleeping Beauty finally woke up. Maybe Evan was the poison apple, but I broke out of my slumber. I'm stronger. I'm not a victim and I'm not a fool and I don't blame it all on him. I let him do porn. I encouraged it. But we agreed he'd only do it for a few years. I changed my mind. I changed my path. I changed my priorities and he refused to change with me. I'm a different person now. What I once thought was OK is no longer OK. What I once wanted, I don't want anymore. And that's OK. That's natural. It is called growing up and truly finding yourself, and I truly found myself with the help of Evan and my family.

I know what to do now. I still believe in love and will marry again, but I want it to be a traditional marriage. That doesn't mean I won't marry another rock star, but I'll be smarter about it next time. I know I want to keep Teravision going, but we will eventually have to evolve the company because I don't think Evan and I will be able to continue a healthy working relationship together.

Mistress Couture, though, is 100 percent mine and Debra is helping me run it. It's under my new Tera Patrick LLC in Las Vegas, where I now solely live. We plan to expand the line this year and I can't wait! I also have my new burlesque show called "Sexy," which will debut at a club in Vegas on Valentine's Day 2010. It will be an hour-long burlesque show starring me with a troupe of eight sexy dancers. It's like Cirque du Soleil acrobatics meets the Forty Deuce burlesque dancer. That's right, we have burlesque aerialists in sexy lingerie. I've always wanted to be a Vegas showgirl, and now is the time to fulfill that dream. I've always loved my feature dancing gigs and will continue to hit the stage for that. I also want to write another book (or two, or three) and get back to writing a sex or love advice column like I once did for *FHM* (UK) and *Genesis*.

Evan is no longer my manager. I have a new management team and they want to continue what we started in mainstream and take me to even greater heights. The sky's the limit! They told me I didn't capitalize enough on the crossover that started in 2006 with that *FHM* cover and all of those mainstream opportunities. They told me, "You are a sex icon and should be branded as such. You are not a tragedy. You are a success story, but that story is not over."

Another new direction I want to go in is motherhood. I want kids. We couldn't do it in our marriage with our lifestyle and jet-setting ways. Maybe I can do it now, in a more traditional life with a more traditional man. I can't wait to remarry and give my heart and soul to someone who wants what I want. I won't sacrifice my needs ever again.

We love and respect each other enough to know that our individual growth and happiness are more important than fighting to stay together to make compromises that either of us just can't live with. People change. We changed. We have made compromises and sacrifices in our lives and marriage, but we're at a juncture where the compromises or sacrifices would change who we are and what we want to such a degree that only resentment would result.

It may seem sad, but ultimately it's an amazing gift to help someone awaken their true desires and figure out what they truly want in life. We gave each other that gift of self-fulfillment. And now, strengthened by years together in a loving, supportive relationship, we must continue on apart.

Writing this book with Carrie was like therapy. She made me dig deep inside myself, examine why I've done what I've done and what the emotions were behind it. It brought up the good and the bad and awakened something in me. It also helped me reconnect with Mom and think about what the next chapter in my life may be. I'm excited about the future, the great unknown, but I'm no longer fearful to go it alone. By writing about some intense situations in my life and really analyzing them for the first time, getting to the "why" of it all, it made me feel stronger than I ever have. Looking back, I've lived and experienced some of the best and worst, and I wouldn't change any of it. It made me who I am. It also taught me that it's not over; it's far from over. I don't think it'll ever be over. I'm excited to take on the next adventures.

The bottom line is that I know I can do anything on my own now. I plan to cover my tattoo that says "Evan's Princess." A princess is usually a damsel in distress who needs a Prince Charming to sweep in, save her, and make her happy. I needed that at the time, but I'm no damsel in distress anymore. And I will never be someone else's "princess." I am the queen of my own domain now, and I feel on top of the world for having discovered that.

My Essential Movies

Aroused (1999)

Fire and Ice (1999)

Pick-Up Lines 45 (1999)

Crossroads (1999)

Caught in the Act (1999)

Caribbean Undercover (1999)

Up and Cummers 73 (1999)

Foot Lovers Only (1999)

Farmer's Daughters Do Beverly Hills (1999)

Gallery of Sin (1999)

Girls of Penthouse 4 (2000)

North Pole 11 (2000)

Penthouse Pets in Paradise (2001)

Collision Course (2004)

Tera Tera Tera (2004)

Reign of Tera (2005)

Test Drive (2005)

Appetite for Destruction (2006)

Reign of Tera 2 (2006)

SeXXXpose (2006)

Tera Patrick's Fashion Underground (2006)

Teradise Island: Anal Fever (2006)

Where the Boys Aren't 18 and 19 (2006)

Tera Patrick Is . . . Flawless (2007)

InTERActive (2007)

Tera Goes Gonzo (2008)

Teradise Island 2 (2008)

Sex in Dangerous Places (2009)

You can go to TeraPatrickStore.com to purchase my movies, become a member of TeraPatrick.com for access to my movies for free, or check out www.TeraTrailers.com to get a sneak peek.

Awards

2000: Hot D'Or, Best American New Starlet

2000: XRCO Awards, Best New Starlet

2001: Adult Stars *magazine's Consumer Choice Awards, Best New Starlet*

2001: AVN Awards, Best New Starlet and Best Interactive DVD (Virtual Sex with Tera Patrick)

2001: Genesis *magazine, Best New Cummer*

2001: FOXE Awards, Video Vixen

2002: AVN Awards, Best Tease Performance (Island Fever) *and Best Renting Title of the Year* (Island Fever)

2003: FOXE Awards, Female Fan Favorite

2004: Genesis *magazine, Porn Star of the Year*

2004: FOXE Awards, Female Fan Favorite

2005: FOXE Awards, Female Fan Favorite

2005: Genesis *magazine, Porn Star of the Year*

2006: Genesis *magazine, Porn Star of the Year*

2006: Temptation Awards, Best Actress and Best New Studio (Teravision)

2007: Genesis *magazine Porn Star of the Year*

2007: F.A.M.E. Awards, Favorite Female Starlet

2007: eLINE Awards, Best American Actress, Best Performer and Best Businesswoman

2007: Adultcon Awards, Mainstream Crossover Star of the Year

2008: AVN Awards, Best Cinematography (Tera Patrick's Fashion Underground), *Best High End All Sex Release* (Teravision's Broken) *and Best Interactive Movie* (InTERActive)

2008: F.A.M.E. Awards, Favorite Female Starlet

2008: eLINE Awards, Best Lingerie Label (Mistress Couture)

2009: AVN Awards, Hall of Fame

2009: F.A.M.E. Awards, Favorite Female Starlet and Favorite Star Website (www.TeraPatrick.com)

2009: XBIZ Awards, Crossover Star of the Year and ASACP (Association of Sites Advocating Child Protection) Annual Service Recognition Award

ACKNOWLEDGMENTS

I would like to thank, first and foremost, my family, who have been there for me from the beginning with unconditional love and support: Debra—my best friend, soul mate, and sister—and her husband Daniel; my mom Preeya, who I learned a lot from; my three four-legged babies—Chopper, Mr. Big Time, and Tiger; my nieces Kaila and Madison; my other siblings Matthew and Katie; my dad David; and my stepmother Kara Ostrom.

I could not have done with this without my book team, especially my writer Carrie Borzillo, who went on my entire life journey with me. You know me backward and forward, and I don't know if that's a good thing, but I love you forever and it just keeps getting better. Thank you to everyone at Gotham and Penguin, including my editor Patrick Mulligan, William Shinker, Lindsay Gordon, Lisa Johnson, and the entire staff who are working tirelessly to make this book a success. Thank you to my managers Chris Lighty and Amrita Sen from Violator Management, my literary agent Marc Gerard at the Agency Group, and my attorney David Adelman.

Margaret Cho, I couldn't have asked for a more moving foreword. It touched my heart and you are a true inspiration. Dave

Navarro, Carmen Electra, and Larry Flynt, thank you for the kind words. And Larry, I thank you and *Hustler* for your support.

To my amazing Teravision staff over the years, thank you for helping me make my dreams come true: Max Padilla, Mike Abdelnour, Robert Mora, Candace Kang, and my publicist April Storm.

I also owe a lot to the countless magazines that have put me on their covers or in their pages—*Playboy, Penthouse, Hustler, Genesis* (especially Dan Davis), and *FHM* (especially editor Sam Barclay and photographer Perry Hagopian, who shot my crossover cover). And, to the organizations that have awarded me for me work over the years. I am truly honored.

I'd also like to thank my friends, colleagues, coworkers, photographers, directors, and supporters who have believed in me and helped make my dreams come true (or just kept me sane during the insanity): Jessicka Addams; Anneli Adolfsson; Rebekka Armstrong; AVN for inducting me into the Hall of Fame, letting me host the show, and putting me on countless covers; Andrew Blake; Lisa Boyle; Darius at the Red Parrot (the most amazing club ever); DJ Hideo; Carla Drake; Lisa Boyle; Ricardo Feressi; Lee Garland; Alexandra Greenberg at the Mitch Schneider Organization; Lizzie Grubman; Helenke; Steve Hirsch at Vivid; Ivan Kane of Forty Deuce; Crystal Knight; Delia Kourvatos; Chi Chi LaRue; Lena; Liinda Garristo; Tony Lee of The Lee Network; Juliet Lowrie; Perry Margouleff; Lisa Massaro; Morning Sun's Joe; Myuk; James McDaniel; Ann Myers; Caroline Pace; Michael Politz; Suze Randall; Jason and Raffelina Reyes; Erik Rudd; "Sandy" from AA; Kerry Simon; Charmane Star; Jim South; Tao's Jason and Noah; Paul Thomas; Autumn Weber; my webmasters Claude and Magalie; Teri Weigel; Tovaris Wilson; and Yumi.

Last, I would like to thank Marilyn Monroe, Bettie Page, and Paulina Porizkova for inspiring me. And to my wonderful fans around the world, you humble me and you will forever be in my heart.

Photo Credits

All photos are courtesy of the author except for the following:

Page 36   Lisa Boyle

Page 57   Tera Patrick

Page 58   Tom Fekse

Page 70   Evan Seinfeld

Page 84   Evan Seinfeld

Page 88   Evan Seinfeld

Page 92   Teravision Inc.

Page 96   Suze Randall

Page 97   Reproduced by Special Permission of PLAYBOY Magazine. © 2002 by *Playboy* magazine.

Page 98   Reproduced by Special Permission of PLAYBOY Magazine. © 2002 by *Playboy* magazine.

Page 100   Lisa Boyle

Page 106   Lisa Boyle

Page 115   AVN Publications

Page 138   Ben Hoffman

Page 152   Jon Kopaloff

Page 163   Lisa Boyle

Page 164   Lisa Boyle

Page 176   Jimmy D., Teravision Inc.

Page 186   Lisa Boyle

Page 189   Anneli Adolfsson

Page 204   Evan Seinfeld

Page 215   Evan Seinfeld

Page 219   Teravision Inc.

Page 220   Ben Hoffman

Page 225   Timothy Greenfield-Sanders

Page 226   Lisa Boyle

Page 232   Anneli Adolfsson

Page 235   Evan Seinfeld

Page 245   Artist: Masa at Three Tides Osaka

Page 246   *Bizarre* Magazine (UK)

Page 254   Jon Kopaloff

COLOR INSERTS:

Page 1   Michael Vincent

Page 2   Josh Ryan

Page 3   Josh Ryan

Page 4   Lisa Boyle

Page 5   Lisa Boyle

Page 6   Michael Vincent

Page 7   Michael Vincent

Page 8   Josh Ryan

Page 9   Josh Ryan

Page 10   Evan Seinfeld

Page 11   Reproduced by Special Permission of PLAYBOY Magazine. © 2002 by *Playboy* magazine.

Page 12   Josh Ryan

Page 13   Josh Ryan

Page 14   Josh Ryan

Page 15   Chris Fortuna

Page 16   *Bizarre* Magazine (UK)